Happily Ever After...

A Creative Collection For Children

Edited by Claire Tupholme

forward**poetry**

First published in Great Britain in 2011 by:
Forward Poetry
Remus House
Coltsfoot Drive
Peterborough
PE2 9BF
Telephone: 01733 890099
Website: www.forwardpoetry.co.uk

Foreword

Happily Ever After ... A Creative Collection For Children is the engaging result of our latest competition, designed as a platform for writers to use their creative skills to fashion poetry and short stories specifically to delight the eager minds of the young generation. Forward Poetry are delighted to be able to award the overall winner £200 in self-publishing vouchers with Proprint and gift them, plus the four runners-up, with a free copy of the anthology.

With the aim to inspire children to gain enjoyment and excitement from reading, and listening to others read to them, this anthology boasts a wide variety of creativity, including poetry that employs memorable rhyme and rhythm (great for reading aloud!) and stories that weave whimsical characters with spirited plot lines to create short, engaging tales they can easily relate to.

A shining example of the gift literature can be for children, *Happily Ever After ...* is brimming with stories to spark their imaginations and take them on an adventure, fun rhymes to make them laugh, cleverly crafted morals, and simply light-hearted tales to stimulate dreams at bedtime.

Created by a variety of talented pens,
Happily Ever After ... will appeal to children of all ages - including the perpetual child in all of us!

Contents

The Poetry
&
Creative Writing

Mary The Repairy Fairy

This isn't a story about a land far, far away from a time long, long ago.
It's a story about a girl from a nearby town who, this Christmas, is very low.

Her pet, Robert the rabbit, or Bob the bunny to his friends, is poorly and in pain.
When Mabel, the little girl, cries her Dad promises her that Bob will be right as rain.

Not many children know, including Mabel, that when you cry you release a fairy,
And when Mabel cries for Bob the bunny, she frees a Repairy Fairy called Mary.

The magic happens when Mabel's first teardrop of an unkept promise falls to the ground.
With a twinkle and a spark, Mary bursts forth from the teardrop, leaving Mabel spellbound.

Mary is the Fairy for Fulfilment of Unkept Promises that make children weep.
Her job is to pick up and mend the pieces when parents make promises they can't keep.

Mary the Repairy Fairy spends most of her year lonely, in a box in the loft.
But, at Christmas time, she gets dusted down and there upon the Christmas tree she sits aloft.

When alone at the top of the house she is free to work magic to make dreams come true.
But as the Christmas fairy at the top of the tree she can't as she is in full view.

Oh, what to do . . . Mabel and Bob need help and Mary must find a way to make Bob better.
She has a think and sets in motion three courses of action . . . starting with a letter.

As the house sleeps and all is quiet, she writes with fairy dust by the light of the moon.
Mary's note asks the Christmas Star to shine over Bob tonight to help him get well soon.

The Christmas Star hangs brightly over Bob, sprinkling stardust upon his home all night long.
When morning breaks, and Bob the bunny is still sick, Mary knows that something is still wrong.

That night, when all the lights are off and the Christmas decorations have stopped glistening,
Mary whispers a message to her friend in the attic, knowing that she's listening.

The Christmas Angel, stowed away in the rafters, not chosen this year to top the tree,
Stirs as Mary summons her to help fulfil the duty of the Repairy Fairy.

Mary asks Angel, as darkness lingers, to watch over Bob as he fights his illness,
Angel swoops down, flutters her wings, driving away the germs within . . . then, in the stillness
. . .

Glorious, glittery snowflakes start to fall as the winter sun rises in the sky.
Bob awakes, still poorly, and Mabel starts to cry for fear that her gorgeous Bob may die.

The Repairy Fairy knows that her work to fix Mabel's broken wish is not yet done.
She's had help from the Christmas Star and Angel and now her chances are down to one.

After the day's snowfall and the children's delight in creating a snowman anew,
Mary knows what to do and who to ask and how to make Mabel's unkept promise come true.

At nightfall, Mary needs the help of the big, icy snowman sitting upon the lawn.
She asks him to feed Bob his carrot-nose so its healing powers of magic are born.

The next morning, Bob awakes with the lark and springs from his bed - ready, willing and able.
There's just one person he can't wait to see, the greatest girl ever, his best friend, Mabel.

Charlotte O'Leary

Winner!

Massive congratulations to Charlotte.
Your creative poem was our favourite from the whole collection. You have
won £200 in Proprint self-publishing vouchers and a copy of this anthology.

Well done!

The Monster Who Lived Up In The Mountain

Last night the monster came down the mountain and took another child. The child was unaware that he was being taken by the monster. The child had stopped smiling because his dad had gone on business away from home. Dad, who played with him, hugged him and took him to fun places. Dad, who fed him, bathed him, told him stories, made him laugh and put him to bed.

Now that Dad was away the child was sad. The monster was nurtured by a child's sadness. He loved the taste of a child's tears, it made the monster grow big. The sound of a child's low heartbeat made the monster grow bigger. The smell of a child's sobs made the monster grow huge. The miserable look on a child's face made the monster enormous.

He became so powerful and courageous that he was about to consume the child completely when there was the sound of the key turning in the front door.

The child stopped sobbing, the monster started to deflate. The child's dad stepped inside, the child's tears dried. The monster became so small that he was hardly visible. The child's heartbeat started to race with excitement. Dad picked him up, he felt so tall as if he could touch the sky.

The monster faded away.

Foqia Hayee

Runner-up

Congratulations, Foqia.
Your story wins you a copy of this great anthology.

The Frightening Tale Of Boris Bold

There was a little boy called Boris Bold,
Who was naughty and rude - he never did as he was told,
He called his sister bad names and made her ever so sad,
When he flushed her doll down the toilet - he just loved being bad!

Boris smiled when he put a spider on his teacher's chair,
And laughed out loud when she screamed, as she jumped up in the air,
He smirked when he put itching powder in his daddy's pants
And giggled as he yelled, 'Watch out for the ants!'

It didn't matter who he tricked, Boris didn't care,
He even spread jam on the headmaster's chair!
He didn't listen to his mam warn he'd go too far one day,
And a wicked witch would come and whisk him away.

One day Boris came across a black cat on a wall,
It would be such fun just to push it, and then watch it fall!
He shoved it hard, but to his amazement, it didn't even twitch
And to his horror it changed shape - it turned into The Witch!

Boris tried to run, but his feet were stuck fast to the ground!
He tried to shout for help, but his words came out with no sound,
The Witch cackled at Boris, and hissed full of glee:
'Little boy, you're so bad, you remind me of me!'

Boris started to cry when The Witch roared:
'Now speak -
I need a bad child, one I can keep,
Will you come with me now? You don't need to be sad,
Just think, Boris, you will always be bad!'

But all Boris could think of was his mum at home, making food,
His dad playing games with his sister, of everything good,
He didn't want to live with The Witch or be bad anymore,
So he got on his knees and began to implore:

'I'm sorry Mrs Witch, for what I've done,
I thought being bad would always be fun,
But I know now I was wrong, and I don't mean to be rude,
I just want to go home to my family and start being good!'

The Witch snarled at Boris:
'Bah! You said sorry you fool!
I can't take you now; I can't break the rule -
I don't need somebody good; I need nasty and bad,
But if you're so naughty again, I'll get you, my lad!'

Suddenly Boris could run, and he raced back to his house,
Where he sat down to his dinner, as quiet as a mouse
After the meal he even helped to clear the plates away,
Now Boris behaves well and is happy - every day!

Anneliese Paterson

Runner-up

Congratulations, Anneliese.
A copy of this book is on its way to you.

Harriet's Hayfever

Harriet the elephant was walking one day,
In the forests of Thailand, a long way away,
She saw some pink flowers and without thinking, put
Her long grey nose right into a bud.
She forgot of her allergy,
And that short little whiff,
Turned into an extremely long, glorified sniff.
Her nose started twitching and itching and popping,
She knew what was coming and wouldn't be stopping,
With tissue ready and the area cleared,
She hoped it wouldn't be as bad as she feared.
She tied herself down to the root of a tree,
And counted backwards, starting from three.
'Here it c . . . c . . . comes!' she quietly stuttered,
Word got around and everyone scattered.
'Atishoo!' she did sneeze and from out of her nose,
Shot bogies and snot and a dog with ten toes!
A wrinkled old wizard with a black and white cat,
An orang-utan in a pink bobble hat!
Three white mice and two rainbow fishes,
Six dinner plates and four pudding dishes!
Then a hundred sardines all squished in a tin
With another outside crying, 'Let me come in!'
A hairdresser's brush and a barber's comb,
And one little pig trying to find his way home.
A 747 jumbo jet,
And thirty-three sea slugs all slimy and wet!
Four cheeky boys making a horrible noise,
And five giggly girls admiring their pearls.
A scientist's brain,
A blue gecko's tongue,
And a yellow canary singing a song!
A leather purse made from an old sow's ear,
And a bag of chips she'd eaten last year,
'Oh dear,' cried the Harriet,
And fell to her knees,
'I wish I hadn't done such an enormous sneeze!'

Margaret Day

Runner-up

Congratulations, Margaret.
You are our fourth runner-up and will also receive a copy of the book.

John The Duck

There once was an ugly duckling
Who lived on a pond in Slough
But the one thing this duck wanted
Was to stand in a field as a cow

He never had a flair for flying
For quacking and eating bread
He'd rather graze in the fields by day
And at night sleep in a cattle shed

Now this duck, we'll name him John
Never had any fellow feathered friends
Because all his mooing and eating grass
Would drive them round the bend

So they kept a wide berth of our pal John
Never asked him to join them play
But, 'Oh I don't care, moo moo moo!'
Was all he'd choose to say!

When one day it came to him . . .
A light bulb above his head
'Rather than staying in my watery home
I'll live on the grass instead!'

'That's what cows do!' he said to himself
A broad grin spread across his bill
'Now to find a nice green patch
I think there's one over that hill!'

So off he went to start a new life
With his twenty new moo-ing mates
Whether this was a good idea
It's up to you to debate

He's been there for 10 years now
I am sure you won't believe
I guess in order for you to understand
For yourself you'll have to see

So if you go to that field in Slough
I can tell you, you'll be dumbstruck
When you see twenty cows chewing the cud
And one happy moo-ing duck!

Runner-up   Zoe Brown

Zoe, you've won a copy of this book as we loved your poem too.

~ 7 ~

Christmas Time - It's Christmas

Christmas time is here again,
Snow has fallen, the days are cold.
The shops look lovely with their decorations.
Father Christmas visits the high street.
Beautiful presents are here for sale.
Christmas trees adorn the streets.
Mummy has decorated every room.
Christmas cards begin to arrive,
We hear from relatives once again.
On Christmas Eve 'tis with us now,
We go to bed early.
Tomorrow morning we will rise early,
Thank you Father Christmas for the promise to visit us.

Janet Cavill

Fighting

He fought and fought with all his might,
He fought and fought day and night,
He thought he fought to do what was right,
But really he fought just to fight!

Charlotte Kiker

Crazy Colours

The colours were so bright way up in the sky
It made you feel happy and wished you could fly
But one day a great storm made the sky grow so dark
All the children looked up, dogs started to bark.

Even though the colours enjoyed the sun and the rain
On occasions like this, they were under some strain
They changed direction, became terribly confused
Some were befuddled, others bemused.

Ronnie Red, alas bashed his poor head
And spent a long week curled up in his bed
Olivia Orange, so radiant and bright
Turned much paler when she got a fright
Yasmin Yellow was an angry young fellow
Who lost his temper before he could mellow
Georgie Green swallowed a broad bean
And grew so tall he couldn't be seen
Bobby Blue caught a feverish flu
And sneezed for days before he knew
Ilona Indigo suffered from vertigo
And had many an hour not knowing where to go
Victoria Violet became a pseudo pilot
Looped the loop and became Veronica Violet.

But soon all was well, with the colourful crew
As they joined together to create a spectacular hue
A rainbow that stretched from the Earth to the sky
Displaying such beauty, a delight to the eye.

Liam Heaney

Tiger, The Metal Detecting Cat

'Oh, I love metal detecting; I can smell some just about here. *Sniff,* that's it; I'm right on the spot. I hope it's a fish flavour can of cat food.

Trevor's spotted me pawing the ground and now he's heading straight toward me, sweeping his detector over the surface.

Oh hurry and dig it up; I can almost taste the food.

Oh what! Is that it? Just an old silver thimble some farmer's wife dropped.

Sigh! I'm not a happy tabby. I'll just lick my paws until I can think of what to do next.

Hey! There's a rabbit, I could do with some exercise, so I'll chase him. Oh nice rabbit, don't run away, let me catch you.

You won't get away now; I've got you trapped down this hole.

Bump! Clumsy rabbit, why did you stop? I might have hurt myself running into you like that.

Who lives here? Phew! It's very smelly down here in the dark.

Oi, why are you leaning so hard on me?

Heck! Why are those two big eyes staring at us?

My butt's wiggling now, I'm so scared. (Shiver)

Let's slowly back our way out toward the entrance. Then run, before that fox eats us both.

Ugh *thud!* I've tripped over something which is sticking out of the ground.

Crumbs! It's such a posh can and looks like real gold; this must have belonged to the Roman emperor's cats.

Purr, I wonder why my family's making such a fuss of me?'

Josie Smith

The Day The World Got Warmer

Mandy the mammoth was munching some chewy leaves. Suddenly she shivered. A cold wind had sprung up. She looked around, over the vast plain, to the distant mountain. It had a dent in the top. Recently, rumbles came from it. Sometimes smoke and even bright, glaring fire.

There was a loud bang. Mandy stopped chewing. She sniffed the wind, now hotter, smelling of ash. The mountain was burning and the ground underneath her was shaking. She yelled for her mother. 'Mama!'

Another small creature was running fast towards Mandy. A very peculiar animal. Covered in hair, with fingers and toes instead of paws. It whimpered in fear.

Mandy moved towards it as it collapsed. In pity, she nuzzled it with her trunk as hot sizzling fireballs hit the ground nearby. Ashy, sparky rain stung.

'You're human, aren't you?' she asked. The little boy nodded, as if he understood mammoth language.

Mandy scooped him up and put him on her back. Together they rushed for safety. But the volcano was not finished. Clouds of sulphur shot from its broken top. Mandy saw another mammoth running and hailed her friend, 'Hi, Tanya, come with us!'

Tanya replied, 'I thought something might happen. The wind has smelled funny for days, and the ground in my den keeps shaking. The birds keep going around in circles and screeching. They usually know before anyone. I bet *you* didn't know the mountain is a volcano!'

Pamela Harvey

Moles

(For our grandchildren Merry Millie, Cheerful Charlotte and Happy Harry)

Moles dig holes.
Everybody knows moles dig holes,
and some moles dig holes faster than others.

Some moles have dug so many holes
they're into double digits.
The fastest double digit digger
is undoubtedly our Doug.

Doug digs double digit holes so fast
he's dug it (and it's made to last)
before other diggers even start.
Many diggers think it is because
he's got a bigger ticker.

The whole hole digging brotherhood
had a competition
to see who was the fastest double digit digger
in the whole hole digging community.

Doug and many other started digging
double digit holes.
The other double digit hole diggers
were demoralised from the start.
Our Doug was digging diligently,
sure he was going to win.

Doug was still doggedly digging
when he found he was backed up
against the backside of Brock the Badger.
Brock the Badger's brush was blocking
Doug's double digit digging race -
and poor Doug lost!

But everyone knew he would have won
if Brock the Badger's brush hadn't blocked
Doug's double digit digging.

David Walter

Lucky Number

Three horns on display has Triceratops,
(Three is his lucky number),
Wherever he sees water, there he stops.
Scores of dinosaurs outnumber
Old Three Horns - for that is what all call him -
While he expects them to queue behind him.

A cheeky Pterodactyl heard to scream,
'You've had more than enough to drink!
Your three horns are out of someone's bad dream,
With thick pillars for legs, you'd sink
Should you fall in while admiring your face
But, at least, that would leave others some space . . .'

Triceratops lifts three horns high
And his growl becomes a holler.
Pterodactyl can dodge - as well as fly -
And screams, 'As for your daft collar,
With those three horns, the thing just looks silly.
With fat legs, avoid anything frilly.'

Pterodactyl stirs up that thirsty queue,
All blame Three Horns for the delay.
Some are inclined to ridicule him too -
But, suddenly, they hear him say,
'Three Horns, forgive and forget what I said.
If that huge T-rex grabs you, you are dead!'

Triceratops thrusts his three tusks forward.
This stops huge T-rex in his stride.
He knows Old Three Horns will not budge a yard.
He takes one moment to decide . . .
No he will not fight Three Horns yet again -
He leaves - despite Pterodactyl laughter.
Here, dinos drink happily ever after.

C M Creedon

Caught By Chance

I caught a tiger by the tail
But to no avail
Let out such a wail
I knew I'd fail
And go to jail
By email.

He looked a bit pale
Just like a white whale
Up and down dale
He told such a tale
Whipped up like a gale
He'll have to go on sale.

I looked in the mail
Bag hooked on a nail
Brought in by a snail
And unhappy quail
Rushed by monorail
On stones of frozen hail.

This tiger male
Drank a pint pot of ale
Before it went stale
Dragged over the shale
With straw in a bale
In a well hidden vale.

Pauline Pickin

Jimmy Harris' Day Out

Little Jimmy Harris was sitting in the car
His mum and dad kept telling him it wasn't very far
They were going on a trip to the seaside for the day
And after only half an hour, Jimmy Harris had to say
'Are we nearly there yet? Have we far to go?
Can we paddle in the sea? I really need to know.'
Mum and Dad just smiled at him and told him not to worry
'We'll be there soon enough; there is no need to hurry.'
'But I want to build a sandcastle and eat a big ice cream
And fly my kite up in the sky and hear the seagulls scream.'
'All in good time, Jimmy,' Dad said to his son
'We're going to be there very soon, and then we'll have some fun.'
They finally arrived and headed for the sand
Jimmy ran on fast ahead with his bucket in his hand
'I'm going a build a sandcastle, the biggest ever seen
Then I'll build two great big towers with a moat that runs between.'
When he'd finished off his castle he began to fly his kite
He held on to the string and ran until his kite took flight
It rose up high into the air, higher and higher it flew
'Look Mum, look Dad, it's almost out of view!'
The day went very quickly and soon it was time to go
And in the car, Jimmy leaned his head up against the window
'I've had a lovely day,' he said happily whilst yawning,
'I wonder if my sandcastle will last until the morning?'
It wasn't long before it grew dark, and Jimmy fell asleep
He'd had a very busy day with happy memories to keep.

Lynne-Marie Perkins

Bog Man Of Denmark

Cautionary tale of The Bog Man of Denmark
Lay dead in the bog
Till one day The Bog Man was found

Historical findings
Glad tidings
So grand

The Bog Man of Denmark
Lay deep
In the bog, they dug him up

Bog Man of Denmark
Take off our hats
Stories told about The Bog Man of Denmark

The tale of The Bog Man of Denmark
A handshake
From the past

A scary sight
Children took fright
Listening to the tale of The Bog Man of Denmark

Poor Bog Man of Denmark
Touched our heart
Today children stay happy

The Bog Man of Denmark
Dug out from the bogs
Lives on in memory

I took the spade
I dug it up
Thrilling all children

Really was real
Children now carry on smiling . . .
At the tale of The Bog Man of Denmark.

S M Thompson

The Saturn Sprite

At Christmas Eve seek out the sprites
Of jaundiced flesh and bloodied spikes
Dark wings *sleek-sharp* as forest holly
Perched on pyracantha jolly
For Saturn's sprites do thrive on snow
But *bitter* their intent, you know!
They jive on pipes to freeze them hard
And ice the street and frost the yard
They tear your coat and snag your scarf
And rob your sleep and steal your laugh
For Saturn's sprites are spirits cruel
Though if you spy one, as a rule
He'll smile the broadest grin you'll see
To test your heart's sincerity
At this, 'the season of goodwill
To all men' - whether good or ill
And long before bells chime 'new year'
Those Saturn sprites will disappear
Unless, of course, you've been unkind
And then one happily strays behind
To hear your grumbles, curses, moans
This Christmas time, 'til all alone
You'll find yourself - just you and he
For misery loves company!
Then Saturn's sprite depletes the joys
You might have shared with girls and boys
If *only* you could give without
The tiniest of selfish doubt
That what *you've* gifted to your friends
Is *nicer* than you'll get from them!

Goblet Boodles

King Cat

That Ollie was a titled cat was very plain to all,
But how and where it came about, no one can recall,
There was that special something, seen only by a few,
Most of us were ignorant, but dear old Ollie knew.
    The way he walked imperiously, or strutted, I should say,
    Here comes King Ollie of The Close, padding down our way,
    With black and white coat shining, he really was a sight,
    Whether basking in the sun, or prowling late at night.
But to the present, he's still here, living close to me,
That he's the master of the house is clear for all to see,
Living room, conservatory or maybe window sill,
Rested and relaxed is he, remaining there until
    The pangs of hunger stir his frame, his thoughts are of his meat.
    He wakes his mistress before dawn, for his breakfast treat,
    This proves he is superior, she must obey his call,
    If not, he'll keep on nagging her, she'll get no rest at all.
Outside a cat comes into view, will Ollie stand his ground?
One royal growl's enough to scare, that moggie can't be found,
We salute you dearest *Oliver,* you're worth your weight in gold,
Please stay with us for many years, until you're very old.

J R Jackett

My World

Wind whirls round the dark house,
Sharp rain spatters the windows,
I lie warm and safe in my bed, snugly curled,
In my cosy cocoon turn the key to the dream door
And enter the realm of my own special world.
I'm an astronaut zooming through time and through space,
Finding alien races and planets unknown.
Or I'm hacking my way through a tropical jungle
To rescue a friend who lies hurt and alone.
I can sail the high seas in a tall masted ship,
Fighting pirates and monsters which rise from the deep.
I'm a scientist battling to find a solution,
While plague victims suffer and helpless men weep.
At a racing car's wheel or astride a bold stallion
I travel a world known to no one but me,
Where I make the rules,
Where I'll be what I choose,
Where no one can follow and no one can see.
And though it may fade as I fall into slumber
And drift through the hours to the following day,
The key's safe in my mind and each night in my bedroom
I open the door and once more I'm away.

Ann Warren

When Mommy Takes Me To The Park

When Mommy takes me to the park,
I can play on the slide.
Or maybe see some squirrels,
Before they try to hide.
I can walk among the trees,
Or see clouds up in the sky.
See fish in the stream,
Or chase a butterfly.
I can hear the chirping birds,
Or the singing of a lark.
I can do all this and more,
When Mommy takes me to the park.
When Mommy takes me to the park,
We'll cook hot dogs at noon.
See cute little chipmunks,
Or maybe a racoon.
Play in the tall grass,
Or on a hollow log.
Roast marshmallows,
Or maybe catch a frog.
Pretty soon we have to leave,
Because it's getting dark.
But there's always more adventures,
When Mommy takes me to the park.

Jay Berkowitz

My Chimney Sweep Treasure

We now have a visitor, who has come to stay,
He's made of coloured wools, and I really must say
How smart he looks, although a chimney sweep,
He's so realistic, and he's mine to keep.

He wears a grey cap, which rests on his head,
With blonde curls, just showing, I'm going to call him Fred,
Green is the coloured scarf around his neck,
To trap the soot, when it falls, I expect.

His smart grey trousers blend with his cap,
Busy he's been, his hands and face show smudges of black.
Fred's chimney sweep brush is a master craft piece,
How proud he appears, tight in his grasp with no release.

A charming little visitor, who reminds me of time past,
When coal fires were Heaven sent, I thought meant to last.
But as with so many of life's richest treasures,
Progress means the birth of modern things,
Replacing the coal fire, and its pleasures . . .

Lorna Tippett

Abdul

At night I take novels to bed
And wear a small dog on my head.
His name is Abdul.
He holds a candle
And follows the words as they're read.

Joe Hoyle

The Polar Bears' Party

When I am good
I am very good

When I am bad
I am very bad

But always I try to be bad in the best possible way

Do you like me, wish you could jump into the sea
And create a tsunami?
Or roller skate using two choo choo trains?
Ride a snowboard across the arc of a rainbow?
Play catch with an orang-utan, huh?

In my utopia polar bears would drink ice cold Martinis
In the afternoon sun and talk a dialect similar to us
The people (or animals you may say)
Would communicate in a series of grumbles and grunts
Not audible to the educated folk but only to the likes of us
(Why would a polar bear with a PhD wanna talk to us?)

In my utopia the seals would tell jokes (we could understand
Them cos they're not a lot more superior to us)
The penguins would dance and the gulls would sing
The big giant walrus would make sure no one naughty got in
They would laugh and cheer all through the night
Drinking and telling stories, reliving fights
Then a big stretch and a big *yawwwwwn*
And all the bears' good friends leave to go home
With the cubs all safe and tucked up in their beds
Daddy Bear says, 'Honey put out the man.'

Steven Corlett

Strawberry Jam

Strawberry jam
Will go *blam!*
If you throw it out of the window

If you do that
It will go *splat!*
When you throw it out of the window

Letting it drop
It will go *plop!*
When you throw it out of the window

So strawberry jam goes
Blam!
Splat!
Plop!
When you throw it out of the window

Strawberry jam
Going *blam!*
When it's thrown out of the window

It's not all that
If it goes *splat!*
When it's thrown out of the window

Don't let it drop
And it won't go *plop!*
When it's thrown out of the window

Strawberry jam should only go
Blam!
Splat!
Plop!
If you have toast and it's going on top!

Matthew Lambert

Goldilocks And The Three Bears - An Alternative Rhyme!

Legend says Goldi had lovely locks
And dressed in pretty girly frocks.
But there's more than meets the eye
And this little rhyme will tell you why.
Something about her smelt rather cheesy
Being near her wasn't easy.
The Three Bears cried, 'Pooh, what a smell!
Now listen up we've advice to tell
If you wear your socks for a week
Then you will surely begin to reek.'
Goldi said nought, she didn't reply
She could not answer, could not lie
When her socks were to blame
She could only hang her head in shame
And so her face blushed bright pink
It *was* her feet that caused the stink
And so the moral of this tale
Wear fragrant socks, never stale
Or you will surely end up like Goldilocks
Shown up by a pair of mouldy socks!

Philippa Rae

Down On The Farm

Down on the farm I love to be
With all the great sounds and sights to see
I love the sheep and cows and hens
Even the pigs lying in their pens
My favourite treat is a tractor ride
The giant haystack's a great place to hide
The baby ducks and chicks are so cute
As they try to peck my welly boot
The farmyard cat lazing about in the sun
While the sheepdogs run around having fun
Oh, how I love that smelly old place
It *always* puts a smile on my face.

Stella Mortazavi

Treble The Bird

Treble the bird is a tiny bird
As tiny as a needle pin
Short by a poppy of three
Or below half a stem from two

Treble the bird is a fuzzy bird
Soft as a pillow and pedal
A crown of feathers to brush
And wings that whisper and hush

Treble the bird is the loudest bird
Crows like a rooster in barns
Caws like a raven would caw
Sharp as a whistle and more

Treble the bird is unlike many
For hatchlings grow from tiny eggs
Soon calling chicks to chickens
But not Treble, for he is neither

Treble the bird is a button quail
All grown up fitting your hand
Runs like rain and just as quiet
But be careful, he talks back

Yes, Treble talks back, but not like us
For after all he is a bird
Yet unlike other birds
You can understand Treble

So if ever you understand a quail
Listen to what he has to say
And talk back, because he might just be
Treble the bird.

Eugene Docena

Animal Capers . . .

Dolphin grins and laughs,
Puma paces to and fro
Electric eels, shock!

Cats have cattitude;
Dogged determination
Is the way of dogs.

Every squirrel feels
So bright-eyed and bushy-tailed . . .
Every single day!

A whale of a time
Was had by the cetaceans . . .
What do you expect?

When Christmas comes around
Robin Redbreast likes to pose . . .
For a zillion cards.

Kangaroo's Joey
Wants to bring a friend to tea . . .
But Mum says crumbs itch.

Ants in procession
Bees making a beeline . . .
Both as the crow flies.

Before going shopping
Porcupine writes down a list . . .
With a quill, of course.

Donkey and zebra
Fell in love and had a foal -
They called her Debra.

Horses horse around
Does so dear are female deer
Frogs play games of Leap!

Woodchucks don't chuck wood;
A frog could be Prince Charming -
Foxes are so sly!

Ant struggles uphill,
Lugging a load so heavy,
For the common good.

Chickens in the yard,
Cows grazing in the meadow;
Poor jay in a cage!

Eels swim so sleekly;
Elephants never forget,
Elks are majestic.

Beavers build their dams,
Changing the course of rivers -
And of history, too!

Flies in the ointment:
Butterflies prefer butter;
Kites fly in the sky.

Alone on a floe,
Happiness is a penguin
Unsteady of gait.

Jays sometime jay-walk;
Not all sheep are sheepish;
Some fish are fishy.

Goats smell caprylic;
Geese are extremely silly,
Gophers go for broke.

Lions are the mane thing;
Monk seals lead a sheltered life;
Bees are . . . the bee's knees!

Puma stands alert;
Dormouse sleeps his life away;
March hare doesn't care!

Oyster in the sea,
When asked what the world is like
Says, 'Just like me!'

Peacock struts his stuff;
Mandrills paint their faces;
Zebra wears jim-jams!

The anteater's nose,
And the elephant's trunk -
Pigs' snouts, but longer!

The hyenas laugh;
Crocodiles pretend they're crying;
Jaguars are not cars.

Vexed beyond patience,
The viper and the cobra
Have a hissy fit!

Black and white penguins
Waiting in the queue to dive -
Uniformity!

Tanja Cilia

Dotty

There once was a dog named Dotty,
Who really was quite potty
She'd chase her tail,
Which, without fail,
Always ended up all knotty.

She was black and white and had a pink nose,
Covered in fur from her head to her toes,
Really only quite small,
With a love for a ball,
Always waiting to chase those throws.

Now Dotty had a friend called Kip,
Who was really, really very hip,
A funny little dog,
Similar to a frog,
He always gave a hop and a skip.

These two were the best of mates,
Always ending up in some terrible states,
From rolling in poo,
To chewing a shoe,
They certainly had some fantastic dates.

Marie Date

Little Piggy

Little piggy in the tree
When will you come play with me?
Shall I catch you in a net
Or go and get the local vet?

Little piggy what is wrong?
Why do you stay up there so long?
Do you want to come and play?
So please get down, sometime today!

Little piggy way up there
Looking down without a care
When are you climbing down?
I will make sure that you don't drown!

Little piggy in the tree
I don't believe that you trust me!
But I am waiting in the water
Just as any good chum oughta!

Little piggy come on in
Time to see if you can swim
Please take a dip, just for a while
You'll find me a friendly crocodile

Little piggy takes a leap
Lands on the bank tall and steep
He trots away into the bushes
While I hide in the ballrushes!

Little piggy climbing trees
Likes to eat the tender leaves
This means I have to do without
A meal of trotter, tail and snout!

Trish Campbell

Some Cats

Some cats are ginger,
Some cats are grey.
Some like to sleep,
And some like to play.

Some cats are big,
Some cats are small.
Some are quite fat,
And others quite tall.

Some cats are furry,
Some are short-haired.
Some cats are cunning,
And others quite scared.

Amber Roskilly

Big Mama

When Gran hung out the washing on laundry day,
I couldn't help but stare.
Upon the line for all to see,
The most gigantic pair of underwear.

At first I thought it was a table cloth,
Or a silly looking frock.
But I soon came to realise,
The material was made for large buttocks.

The twins, the pair, the derriere,
Nothing larger can compare.

My mother told me that in this situation,
'Big Mama' would be the polite term to use in conversation.
Easier said than done when that piece of material
Looks like it could house an entire nation.

Sam Carroll

The Good, The Bad And The Ugly

Human beings have basic traits
They nurture their young offspring
With the guardiance of a panda's hand
With the support of a deer's herd
With the comfort of a bear's hug
With the warmth of a kangaroo's hips
With the shelter of a mole's hole
With feeding of milk and honey
Oh taste the sweetness of their care!

Human beings have excesses
They are prone to evil ways
Like the conceited lion on high
Like the greedy pig in a hoard
Like the lazy sloth in the heat
Like the lustful hyena on heat
Like the angry wolf in a huff
Like the jealous man full of hate
Oh smell the death of their misdeeds!

Human beings have special gifts
They display holy virtues
Like the modesty of Jesus Christ
Like the honesty of Moses
Like the courage of King David
Like the wisdom of King Solomon
Like the patience of Abraham
Like the forgiveness of the Lord
Oh see the beauty of their acts!

Eunice Ogunkoya

If I Was Queen

If I was queen of
this here land,
I would rule as in
days of old.
Live in palaces,
proud and stately.
Or dark, foreboding
castles, with dungeons deep.
Protected by soldiers, loyal and true
(or off with their heads it would be!)

Tall, beautiful and proud
I would be.
Dressed in velvet and
in silk.
Maids to meet my
every need.
My every whim to satisfy.
(Or tantrums would ensue.)
Not a finger I need raise.
Yet dearly beloved by all
I would be.

My days filled with fun,
frolicking and fair folk.
Knights jousting and
duelling, me to impress.
Dancing all night,
I would be.
Adored by my husband,
the king.
My every command he would obey.
Or off to the dungeon with him,
it would be.

My subjects may starve
and suffer.
The laws may make
themselves.
Mayhem may result.
But happy, they would be
(or off with their heads it would be).

Dorcas Wilson

Fairy Tale Loves

I am Snow White. Seven dwarfs protect me.
When Prince Charming comes, his kiss awakens me.

I'm Sleeping Beauty. I pricked my finger.
A prince kissed me. His lips, on mine, did linger.

I am Cinderella. After I lost my shoe,
The prince searched for me. We then said I do.

Lady and the Tramp, we set out to dine.
Fell in love with each other. We are canine.

I kissed the ugly beast. My name is Beauty.
He turned back to a prince, who's a cutie.

Just call me Wendy. My love's a young man
Who behaves like a boy, his name, Peter Pan.

My love is Bambi. He's a deer and my beau.
My name is Faline. I am a young doe.

Aladdin, on his carpet, he brings me joy.
I'm Princess Jasmine and nuts for this boy.

I'm Pocahontas. I married a charmer.
His name is John Rolfe, a tobacco farmer.

He calls me Jane. We swing from a vine.
Tarzan the ape man. He knows he's all mine.

I'm Ariel. I've a tail like a fish.
My prince will see legs because that is my wish.

I'm Princess Fiona. He made the trek.
My rescuer, an ogre. His name is Shrek.

Princesses are real, not just in tales.
Like Lady Diana, Princess of Wales.

All of these stories were written for laughter.
But one thing's the same, the love's ever after.

Ana Lorenzo

The League Of Gentledogs

Smovi is a handsome cocker spaniel
He is a blue roan not a bluebell
He has lots of doggy friends
Which he likes to contend

His friend Hombre is a chihuahua
He loves a poodle named Conchita
He said, 'Smovi is a Spanish gringo
Who likes to dance the flamingo!'

Smovi's friend Rover is a Labrador
Who likes to fetch the sticks with furore
With his golden mother Sadie
And his swimming sister Blondie

Smovi one day eloped with Emma a black lurcher
With his crooner's style, he loves very much her
They had a son named Louis
Who is just the replica of his daddy

Louis carries on the story
With his good friend Stumpy
And his half-brother terrier Guinness
They form the league of gentledoggies
Which is a society for the dogs' happiness!

Victorine Lejeune Stubbs

Puppet Love

There once was a young man named Tutty,
Who many considered quite nutty.
One night while asleep,
He has visions of Sweep.
Then woke up and thought he was Sooty.

Paul Kelly

Good-Morning And Good-Night

Our robin thinks he's a nightingale
As just before the light,
He starts his merry singing
Bringing the morning from the night.

Not for us a clattering clock, nor
Reveille from a boisterous brass band,
But the gentle call of a robin.
The very best awakening in the land.

And when the day is ending
And stars begin to appear,
Out of the closing darkness
It's the robin that we hear.

Dinah van der Werf

Sleeping Beauty

Her hair was gold,
And her skin was ivory
Her looks were fine with lips so red -
She was a true beauty.
He was tall with darkened hair
And a scar that marked him true.
She belonged to him and he to her,
This is a tale of prince and maiden fair.

He rode upon his noble steed -
A charge of mighty strength,
Toward her prison he did fly
But from the ground a dragon rose, it reached into the sky;
Our prince, he drew his sword and performed a mighty deed.
He slew the beast in a fearsome fight
Of flames and blades of steel.
He ran up the tallest tower and into a room of light.

Upon the bed she lay - asleep to all the world,
He knelt beside her and brushed aside a curl.
He bent his head to her rose red lips, and a kiss he gave to her.
And to his gentle eyes she woke.
With a whisper soft he spoke
'O maiden that art so fair, I love your rose-red lips
And curl of your golden hair.' Thus she blushed a pretty petal-pink

He took her hand and led her down the stair,
He sat her daintily upon his horse
And toward the sunrise they rode
Off into their happily ever after . . .

Lorna Haines

Insects And Bugs

Hiding in
The flowers,
A spider makes its web,
Delicately laced
In silk,
As fine as thread,

How it glistens
In the sunlight,
Reflecting from the sky,
Shades of
Rainbow colours,
Attracting little flies

So busy
Are the ants,
That march along the ground.
Busy little
Humming bees,
Buzzing all around

Ladybirds
And butterflies,
Resting on some leaves
Slimy slugs
And snails,
Trailing underneath

Hiding under
Flowers, trees,
And even shrubs,
Is where you'll
Find these creatures,
Called the insects and bugs

Barbara C Perkins

The Missing Wishes

Misty the wishes fairy, was so sad that she was crying. Sitting cross-legged on her red toadstool, her pink wings drooped behind her.

'What's the matter fairy?' Hazelnut, the brown fieldmouse asked.

'Oh Mouse,' Misty replied, 'I have lost my three wishes and now there can never be any 'happy endings'.'

'Where did you last see them?'

'I had them in Bluebell Wood and now they are gone,' Misty sobbed.

'Surely all we have to do is retrace your flight path and I am certain that we will find them. But what do three missing wishes look like?'

As she blew her nose on a cobweb hankie and patted down her green gossamer frock, the little fairy replied, 'Well, wishes do sparkle.'

'Brilliant, if they sparkle then we can find them in the dark,' Hazelnut replied.

As soon as night fell, the friends began their search. When they reached Bluebell Wood, Hazelnut stopped.

'What's that over there?' the mouse whispered. 'I can see three tiny pinpricks of sparkling light.'

'You've found them!' Misty cried. 'Quickly, I only have a few more minutes before they lose their power.'

Collecting the wishes on her wand, Misty flew as fast as she could to the home of Holly Jones. It was the little girl's birthday and she had three important wishes to make …

'I wish I could have a puppy. I wish Granny would visit me. But most of all, I wish that everyone would live happily ever after.'

Christina Brooks

Tosey Wins A Rally

Tosey and Banta are a dog and a cat and are best friends. Their owners are a young married couple called the Gywns. Tosey and Banta are always having great adventures!

One day an old rallying friend of Kevin's called up and invited Kevin and his family to watch him race his car at a rally. The pets were coming too as there was no one to look after them at home.

The pets were locked in the car, but the owners had overlooked the fact that they had left a gap in the window of the car that was just wide enough for Tosey the cat to crawl out of.

Tosey strutted round the service area and saw this bright yellow car with flared wheel arches and a spoiler. It was called a 6R4 and was probably the fastest car there. Tosey hid in the yellow car.

The rally started and Tosey loved the feeling as she sped along and, to enable her to see more, Tosey came out of her hiding place. The driver nearly crashed with surprise but decided to finish the rally, with Tosey the cat as his co-driver!

The spectators could not believe their eyes when what looked like a cat arrived in the passenger seat of the winning car. At the end of the rally Tosey was keen to get back to his family.

The Gwyns had been looking for Tosey and, after finding her, had no idea where she had been. So when Kevin read the next edition of his rally magazine he was speechless to see a picture of a rally car with Tosey perched on the dashboard and there was a headline that said: 'The Cat Who Got The Cream! - Scottish Rally Champion wins rally with help from a cat!'

Gavin Mcintyre

Meg And The Red Ball

One day I heard some breaking glass
And I heard our neighbour yell
But exactly what the matter was,
I couldn't really tell.

Then Mr Jones looked over the fence
'Is this your ball?' he said,
'It broke my kitchen window
And hit me on the head!'

'Excuse me, Mr Jones,' I said,
'My ball is soft and green,
That ball which you are holding
Is one I've never seen.

I really think that hard, red ball
Is meant for playing cricket
And as for breaking windows -
Well, I wouldn't be so wicked.'

Just then two boys arrived
To see what they could see
And Mr Jones was very cross,
So I went in to tea.

Hugh Edwards

Happy Ever After

(For Leanne, Georgina and Daniel)

'How far is it to Heaven, will it take more than a day?
Are you happy up there Mummy, do you think that you will stay?
Do you have wings now like an angel or do you twinkle like a star?
If I walked across the rainbow would I get to where you are?'

'Hush my precious daughter! Close your eyes and go to sleep.
Your *dreams* will bring you to me, there's no need for you to weep.
Let them lift you from your slumber, across the Milky Way to glide.
You haven't lost your mummy. I am *always* by your side!

I'm at the end of every rainbow. I'm every star that's up above.
I'm in your heart for always. I have filled it with my love.
I will walk with you through childhood; I will soothe you when you cry.
You will hold me in your memory, I'm *still* here, I didn't die.'

'Oh Mummy, such a lovely dream, you looked so pretty dressed in white!
I want to go back *there* again and see you every night!
Look Mummy on my pillow! Here's the ribbon from your hair!
I'm awake but still I'm dreaming, I can feel you everywhere!'

Lesley Elaine Greenwood

The White Rabbit Is Late

(Inspired by the white rabbit from Alice in Wonderland)

The white rabbit is late
for a very important date
the time won't wait
and I'm oh so late,
no time to dawdle
nor hesitate

please tell me the time
and I'll tell you a rhyme
but not right away
because I'm very late
for a very important date!
I can't make her wait

the queen will have my head
without it I'll be dead
so particular about the clock
and I'm oh so late *tick-tock*
please hurry along; can't wait
no time to hesitate
on the last minute; always late!

Lynne Briers

The Tallest Giraffe

On behalf of myself and my daughter Emma Taff
May I please be permitted to obtain your autograph?
At the same time do allow me to take a photograph
As I need to send this quickly to the Daily Telegraph

This poem of course refers to a very large giraffe
Round whose neck was a polka-dotted brightly coloured scarf
To put this on required a ladder and the zoo's entire staff
And me, hanging round her neck, well! I must have looked quite daft

But not to end this tale too sadly, I write another paragraph
Just to prove after all there's still time to have a laugh
Because there is a 'little secret' I can tell on your behalf
You see that very tall lady, has a very tiny calf.

William Ross

Little Monkey

Why do they always stand and stare?
And poke their noses through the rails
Just when I'm having a nice little nap
They wake me with a rat-a-tat-tat
When I'm swinging from tree to tree
I really don't mind their company
But when I stop to scratch my fleas
I go all shy because they laugh at me
Oh I wish to be wild and free
In the jungle where no one can see.

Margaret Maguire

Mr Snow's Problem

It was winter in Ohnonotagain,
and Mr Weather man had promised snow
all the little children were very excited,

but Mr Snow had a problem,
'I've not enough snowflakes,'
he told Mr Wind sadly,
'I must have miscounted my frosty boxes,
the children, will be so disappointed.'

Mr Wind was a clever chap,
'let's try to sort this out,' he said,

'Well I've a large block of snow
I could grate with my giant grater,
but it's frozen solid.'

'Right, I will fetch Sandra Sun,
she can warm it up,
it will be easier then.'

Sandra arrived, and soon the snow was ready for grating.

Handy Andy arrived
'let me stamp out the flakes for you,' he smiled.

Mr Rain appeared and wanted to help.
Handy put a snowflake mould onto Mr Rain's
rainstick and soon there were lots of snowflakes

Mr and Mr Rainbow Painter came along,
'We will sprinkle glitter on for you.'
'Thank you all,' said Snow
'How would I have managed without you?'

Everyone worked really hard,
soon there were hundreds of frosty flakes
waiting to fall on Ohnonotagain,

'May we all help to scatter the flakes?' asked Sandra Sun,

'Of course,' smiled Snow, 'spread out everyone
then the snow will be deep and even.'

They did exactly that,

soon the boxes were empty,
the sky was filled with hundreds of glittery snowflakes falling
softly and gently, and ah so quietly
on the little town of Ohnonotagain.

Next morning the children were so happy
wrapped up warm and enjoying the snow.

Above in the clouds
everyone smiled,
'Thank you all so much,' smiled Snow,
'We have made the little ones so happy.'

And he was quite right.

J C Davies

Rune The Racoon

This is the story of Rune the Racoon,
his sister Moon and his brother, Boone,
and all the things they put to ruin.

'Be clean and tidy,' their mother cooed.
Since then, they always washed their food.
They cleaned their crumbs and dishes crude.

But when they find your campsite, whoa!
You'll suddenly decide to go:
your food and dishes, dirtied so!

At home, their faces are plain grey.
They put their masks on when they stray,
to disguise who's messiest today.

At night, they even paint their tails,
so they can hide behind the rails;
they sharpen well their small black nails!

At home, they chatter when they play.
When out, they whisper, gleeful, say,
'Who left us all these toys today?'

Were the seats shredded in your car?
Was the trunk popped with no crowbar?
No wipers? Mirrors? They can't be far!

You think your things are safely locked?
Their quickest entry can be clocked!
Your human peace and quiet, mocked!

Ruth Hill

The Horrid Russian Witch

Not long ago a lively young boy lived in a bungalow high on a Welsh hill. He lived with his mum, dad and the princess who cared for him when his mother was ill.

One stormy winter's night, with winds rattling the roof tiles, and wild spirits whispering down the chimney, he lay in bed, but felt safe for he believed that the princess was about to tell him a story with a happy ending.

'Well Raldus! I am going to tell you the story of Mrs Hughes, the old woman living in Gloomy Cottage.'

Raldus remembered the old crone, who stared at him with fiery eyes whenever they passed her garden. She was creepy and scared him.

'Her real name is Lara Ghaghara, who was a horrid Russian witch with iron teeth. She used to live in a little house that ran about on chicken legs, but because of her evil ways the Russians threw her out and she settled into Gloomy Cottage.'

'Why does she wear iron teeth?' asked Raldus nervously.

'To gobble up little Russian boys, and perhaps, little Welsh boys,' she replied with a peal of hysterical laughter.

This was too much for him and closing his eyes, he feigned sleep. Her voice, droning on and on, dissolved, in the whispers of the spirits waiting patiently for him on the rooftop, until there was nothing to hear but the spirits that never stop whispering to him.

Geraldus John

Dream Catcher

Mum was late again. Tom sat on the step outside the school hall and scuffed his clean shoes in the dust. He watched his friends walk out of the playground and soon he was alone.

Once, he would have panicked when the bell rang and there was no sign of her running up the path to meet him, but now he was used to it. He knew if he just waited she would eventually come, red cheeks from rushing, a sad face for being late again. They would hug and she would say sorry, and holding hands, they would walk home through the park, and Tom would be offered ice cream as a way of making up.

Just lately he found that if he daydreamed the time went much more quickly. Today he thought that he would like to be an Indian brave. He closed his eyes and was soon on the plains of America, wrapped in a buffalo robe, practising shooting with a half-size bow and arrow.

He wore a headdress of eagle tail feathers. His house was a wigwam made from a framework of poles covered with bark, rush mats and animal skin.

A dream catcher hung above the entrance. All dreams were believed to come down from the night sky. Bad dreams were captured in the web and held there until the rays of the morning sun melted them away. Good dreams slipped onto the dreamer.

Tom rubbed his eyes and there was Mum.

Beverly Maiden

The Wizard And The Witch

Once upon a time there was a wily Wizard, who liked to tease his friend the Witch.

One day he turned her beautiful black cat into a tiger, which chased her round and round the house.

The Witch was not pleased, so she made a magic spell and turned the Wizard's wand into a lollipop.

The Wizard was not pleased, so he made a magic spell and turned the Witch's broomstick into a bicycle.

The Witch was not pleased, so she made another magic spell and turned the Wizard's hat into an ice cream cone!

The Wizard was not pleased, but he did have a little lick.

'Look here,' he said, 'I am fed up with all your bewitching spells.'

'And I am fed up with your spells,' said the Witch. 'Why don't we do something exciting instead? Why don't we fly with the wind and go round the world?'

'That sounds like a good idea,' said the Wizard, so off they went on the Witch's new bicycle-broomstick!

Shirley Johnson

Candyfloss And Cones

When you close your eyes, can you hear it too?
Bounce, bounce, hoo-hoo-hoo-hoo!
Could it be Tigger? Look, there's Winnie the Pooh,
All your friends have come just to see you.

If you ever feel lonely, just close your eyes . . .
To Narnia you may go.
No White Witch, just Mr Tumnus and Beaver
Along with the most beautiful, pure white snow.

Any time you feel sad, drift off to Neverland,
To get there requires no horse.
Tinkerbell will cover you in pixie dust,
Then you can fly there, of course!

At times you may have doubts,
Only the Wizard of Oz can lighten the load.
The time has come to rest your eyelids,
And follow the yellow brick road!

Noddy will give you some candyfloss,
Or a Teletubby a delicious, multicoloured cone.
Remember your friends are always an eye-close away,
You will never again be alone.

Chris Rye

Mary And The Milky Mouse

Rory McHugh was a tiny mouse
He was only one and he lived in a house,
In Scotland.
Not much of a house
Unless you're a mouse,
But it happened to be on a farm.
The farm had a dairy,
A wonderful thing.
In the dairy was milk
From which came the cheese
Which was sure to please
The tiny mouse who lived in a house,
In Scotland.
On the farm lived a cat
Called Mary McSlatt,
Now the cat liked the milk
And the mouse liked the cheese.
They were easy to please.
Now the cat, at her wish
Drank her milk from a dish.
The dish, it was tin
And young Rory fell in.
The cat fished him out
And gave him a clout,
Well more of a pat,
She was quite an old cat.
Now the cat liked the mouse
And the mouse liked the cat,
So they just became friends,
And that then was that.

Jacqueline Burns

Gobsmacked

Oh my Lord
Gobsmacked is what I've been
When drawing back the blinds
Sitting out there on the green
The biggest toad in all creation
Anyone has ever seen
Like a huge great rock
All knobbly and brown
Right in the middle
Has sat itself down
I rang the local council
They sent a man to look
'Oh my Lord,' he said
And wrote down in his book
Next the local bobbies
Who always walk in pairs
Came to see what they could do
Nothing. Just stand and stare
One to the other said
Have you ever one so large
No indeed was the reply
We must send for the sarge
The poor old toad was getting sick
Of all the gawping going around
So sprouted wings and flew away
Leaving no trace to be found

Daphne Fryer

Alone In The Dark

I don't like 'alone in the darkness'
though my mum says there's nothing to mind,
but what if a tiptoeing sharkness crept up
and he chomped little me from behind?

There's always an alligate grinning
when I lift up the lid of the loo,
Mum thinks that the water will wash him away,
if I flush when I've finished, do you?

A tiger went into our bathroom,
he was terribly scraggly thin,
he only comes out when he wants to be fed,
when he's full up he usually stays in.

He's trying to catch me, I know it,
though Mum tells me he's not really there,
she says I imagine fantastical things
just to give her a bit of a scare.

There are flurks on top of my cupboard,
and umgubbins with candy-striped wings,
you have to look quickly to see them at all,
they are rather invisible things.

I thought I caught sight of a heffant
shambalurkeling under my bed,
I got up my courage and took a quick peep,
and found masses of dust there instead.

A horribly's in my nan's bedroom,
he's got boggling eyes and no hair
and one of his ears has gone missing, a bit,
but the other one's practically there.

Mum promises darkness is friendly,
when she kisses and whispers, 'Goodnight,'
She goes back downstairs when we've finished my read,
but she always leaves one little light.

Rosa Johnson

I Don't Like Spiders

I don't like spiders
I don't like them at all

It doesn't matter
If they're big or they're small

When they arrive
On the scene

I start to yell
And really, really scream

Their legs are covered
In hundreds of little bits of hair

And that's just the
Beginning of my fear

Their bodies are round
And very, very fat

I'm really scared they'll
Explode and go splat!

They have the most horrible
Beady black eyes

They scare me as well
As the moths and the flies

From out of their backside
Comes a sticky web

Imagine that wrapped
Around your head?

I don't like spiders
I don't like them at all

It doesn't matter
If they're big or they're small!

Gaelynne Pound

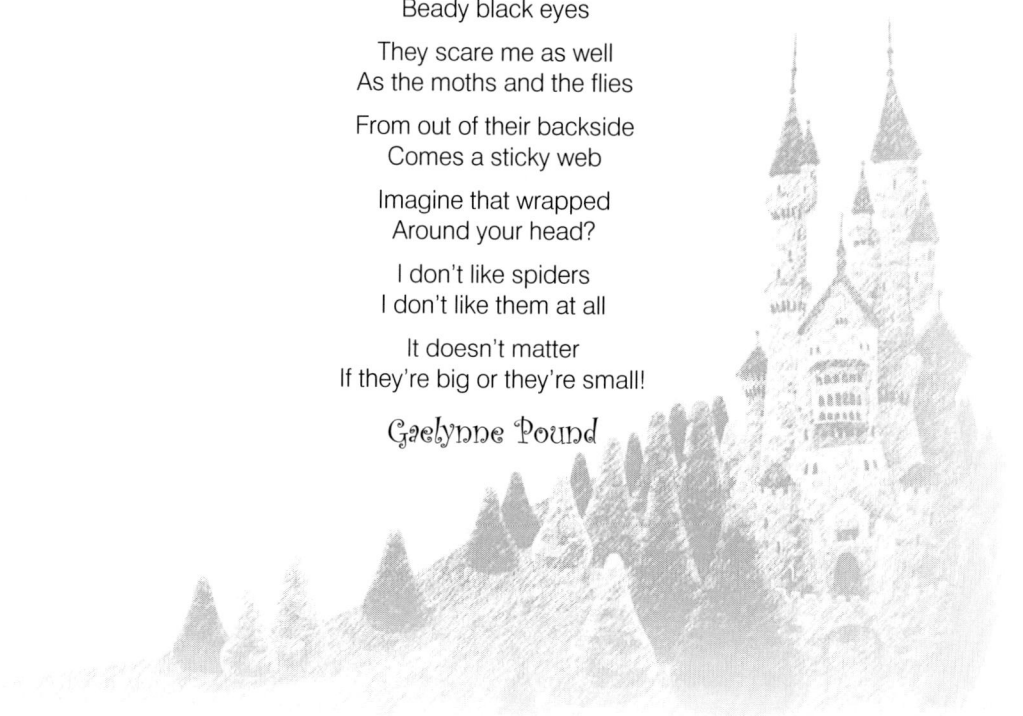

The Wibblywob

Have you seen the Wibblywob,
the wibbly wobbly woo?
The Wibblywob is frightened
is cold and feeling blue.

He curls up in a ball, and is very, very small,
and if you hear . . . the shaking of some knees,
If it is a wibblywob, he'll give a little sneeze.

Then . . . you must sing a song,
a song to calm him down,
you'll know that it is working
when he turns from blue to brown.

Then the Wibblywob will give a great big laugh,
you must take him now to have a nice warm bath.

He'll go from brown to pink,
then a lovely shade of green,
and every other colour that is in-between.

Now he's feeling better
and has some colour in his cheeks,
he'll be your friend forever,
for weeks and weeks and weeks.

Julie Boitoult

The Fish

'I saw a fish wearing a hat.'
'And where did you see that?'

'I saw him swimming in the sea
while I was sipping my cup of tea.

I waved at him and he waved back
and in doing so he lost his hat!'

Noris D'Achille

The Crow And The Cat

Hi, my name is Neelix
And I've been a very, very naughty cat.
It started off when I was sat
In the garden one sunny day,
Sometime in the month of May.

I saw a nest up in a tree,
That's what us cats do you see,
I jumped and grabbed a fluffy ball,
I then leapt down onto the wall.

The mummy crow then squawked and flew . . .
Whatever am I meant to do?
Something took my son away
Now I'll never see him play!

I carried it into the house
Just as I do when I catch a mouse.
My master only said one word . . .
'Neelix!'
As he grabbed and took the bird.

I hadn't hurt the beastly thing
Just a nip above the wing.
He said he'd kill me if I dared
To go anywhere near the precious bird.

He took the bird back to the nest,
He thought that this was for the best.
So this fluffy bird lived to grow
Happily ever after as a crow.

Jill Norris

I'm Flying To The Moon Today

I'm flying to the moon today
In a rocket made of paper,
Bits of string and a worn-out thing,
Past the stars and the Milky Way.
Maybe I'll make new friends there,
Or eat cream cheese on my way.

Do you think there'll be a nursery there?
On that silver bright moon ray
Will there be paint, water, and sand
And a home corner among the planets
Where I can try moon soup of the day?

Is there a place where moon men hide
In a crater full of holes?
Where they watch Moon TV
Or burrow down like moles?

When I've finished on the moon
I'll fly straight home to bed,
Kiss Mum and Dad on the cheek,
And say goodnight to Ted.

Mary Mullett

Space Travel

Charlie Gates didn't know he'd travel far,
As he swallowed some strange sweets from the jar,
Up he went, felt his tiny body rise,
Straight towards the moon - what a big surprise!
He hitched a lift home on a shooting star.

S Mullinger

Hamster

Somebody's stolen my hamster
It was there when I went up to bed
My sister is sitting there laughing
And saying my hamster is dead
She thinks that it's ever so funny
That Hammy keeled over and died
Then she showed me where Hammy was buried
And I dropped to my knees and I cried
The tears only lasted a minute
When a thought entered into my head
If my hamster has gone up to Heaven
Can I have a new puppy instead?

John W Fenn

Helping Mummy

We're helping Mummy to get better
She has a flu and is in bed
We weren't sure if she was sleeping
So we lifted up her eyelids and her head

We're helping Mummy to get better
She has a head hurt and feels sick
We brought her yummy stuff to eat
But she went to the toilet really quick

We're helping Mummy to get better
We wrapped a bandage round her foot
We brought her a flannel just to wipe her
Then sang to her and read her lots of books

Mummy says she really feels much better
She feels so well that we can go to bed
Of course we know she's just being brave
So we'll stay and make her better instead.

Susan Hardy-Dawson

A Fairy, A Gnome, A Frog And A Mouse

Down in the woods in a faraway land
living in a house so very, very grand
live a frog, a fairy, a gnome and a mouse
all living together in this four-bedroomed house
in the dead of night you can hear all sorts of groans and creaks
and little mouse, when he sleeps he doesn't snore, just makes little squeaks
now bright and early when the sun does shine and everyone begins to groan
we can hear the ringing of the telephone
but to the occupants living in this home
can hear nothing but the singing, done by the gnome
it seems to be his morning ritual
don't get me wrong he can sing very well
but he tends to sing rather loud
opera you see, of his voice he is very proud
now the only thing is
on the other end of the telephone is his agent Liz
trying to tell him about a concert
that is being held in the park
they would like for him to sing at the concert in the dark
will he hear the ringing in time?
Will everything turn out fine . . . ?
Fairy hears the phone and rushes to answer it
now if they had missed it, Gnome would have had a fit
but everything is sorted, he is off to fetch his tux
and the feather caps that belong to the ducks
everyone's getting all smartly dressed
and with the singing they will be impressed
they all go out and have a ball
everyone enjoys it, one and all.

Samantha Vaughan

Beach Nuts

With cups of sand
And buckets of shingle
We dance along the beach.
There we hum our tunes
And hide amongst the dunes
Just out of the tide's long reach.

As daylight arrives
And the humans too
We watch with silent breathing.
We whisper in cupped hands
Quietly making up our plans
For when they are all a-sleeping.

Then down we scamper
Towards their hampers
And prise the handles upwards.
We fill our packs
With lots of snacks
Then silently run off backwards.

From in the high dune
We get a good view
As the humans search and ponder.
For their long lost food
Is gone for good
And now they just sit and wonder.

At this funny sight
When we are having a bite
Our giggles make us quiver.
For our mouths are full
And their wine is cool
Such adventuring, such treasure.

Julian Bishop

The Doll's House

Oh, how exciting it would be, if I was really tiny
I could visit the beautiful doll's house of mine,
If I could shrink to squeeze in through the door
I'd be just the right size to play and explore.

I'd rearrange the furniture and sit in comfy chairs
And see what Dolly keeps in the other rooms upstairs,
I'd open up the wardrobe and try on all the clothes
Her dress would fit me very well and she'd take my size in shoes!

I'd play games with the dolls in the nursery
At four I'd lay the table and invite them all to tea,
Then draw the curtains and switch on the lights
How cosy it would be, would *you* like to visit me?

There would be tiny china cups and plates of sandwiches
Before I left, I'd tidy up and put away the dishes,
The mother doll would be out of course! She'd never know I came
Can you imagine the fun *you'd* have being doll-sized for a day?

Sandy Randall

Jockwin The Goblin

This tale is about Jockwin the goblin
A goblin as you know is a tiny wee man
And he loves to practise his magic
As the very best goblins all can

He lived deep in the green forest
In a fairy house by a stream
Happy and safe in the knowledge that
By humans he couldn't be seen

When the local children came to play
And sometimes trample his fence to the ground
He'd get angry and to get his own back
Scare them off by making wild animal sounds

Or he would magic the trees to reach out for them
As they ran here and there at their play
And as the branches would reach out and clutch at their legs
They'd scream in terror and run fast away

As they would run in fear from the forest
He would chase them though they couldn't see
But they would hear his hysterical laughter
As he would caper and dance in his glee

But then when the forest was quiet once more
And just the sound of the birds filled the air
He'd get lonely and long for a visit
Of the children that once more he could scare

Don Woods

The Pound

The pound lay on the ground, not making a sound,
Sparkling away, hoping someone would find him one day,
He felt cold and alone, hoping soon to find a new home,
When all of a sudden a little boy passed by, up came a cry,
'Hey Jack, I've found a pound,'
The pound was whisked up into the air,
Two sets of eyes looking at him with a delighted stare,
'Wow!' said Sam, 'Let's go and show my mum,'
'Come on Slow Coach,' shouted Sam as he started to run,
The pound had found a new friend,
The boy had found some money to spend,
As they ran along the road,
The two little boys thought of what they could buy with the money,
Their thoughts were quite funny,
'I am going to buy a rocket,' said Sam,
As he placed the pound firmly in his pocket,
'So I can shoot up to the moon and stars and maybe even go to Mars.'
Jack thought for a minute then said, 'I am going to buy an aeroplane, so I can visit lots of
countries like Africa, Australia or even Spain.'
The pound chuckled away as he listened to what the two little boys had to say,
If only I could buy them all those things, thought he,
They would need millions more of me,
The pound jiggled up and down happily in Sam's pocket,
As he ran along the street,
Along with a toy car, a few pennies and a sticky sweet,
'Hey Mum, guess what I found?' shouted Sam with delight
And waited to see if his mum would get the answer right,
Sam's mum decided to tease him and play a guessing game,
To see if she could answer the same,
'It is a big tiger that's escaped from the zoo?
Or even a magical dragon or two?'
'No!' squealed Sam, laughing out loud, 'I found a pound,'
Which made him feel very proud,
Sam told his mum what he wanted to buy,
Sam's mum smiled, 'I don't think you will be able to buy all those things,' she said, with a sigh,
'It's nice to be able to dream, but I think you will have just enough to buy you both an ice
cream,
Come on let's take you to the shop, to see Mrs Jolly.'
Sam liked Mrs Jolly, she made him laugh, as she was always funny,
She had a red face and big round tummy,
He thought that one day she would laugh so much she might explode,
Into a million pieces on the road,
When they went in the shop, Mrs Jolly greeted them with a smile,

Then after a little while,
Sam showed her the pound, he had found,
When he told her what he and Jack had thought to buy,
She laughed so loud, Sam thought she would blow the roof off into the sky,
All this time the pound waited patiently in Sam's hand,
Wondering where he would next land,
Soon Mrs Jolly gave Sam and Jack the biggest ice creams you have ever seen,
Sam handed over the pound,
Mrs Jolly put it in her till, where it was safe and sound,
The pound found new friends in the till drawer,
He was happy and content, until he would be on the move once more.

Denise Peach

Camp Out

Alex and Alice were excited, they were going camping. They were on the way home from school, it had been the last day before the summer holidays and they urged Mummy to drive faster so they could get started. Of course Mummy didn't drive faster, she just laughed.

Mummy and Daddy had finally agreed to allow them to camp in the back garden. After all they were only ten.

After tea they collected a sheet, a rope, a pot, knives and forks, plates, torches, a tin of beans, bread and their pyjamas. They went out into the garden and erected their tent, built a fire, cooked beans on toast and eventually went to bed.

They were chatting about whether they would be allowed to go camping again when they heard a loud screech.

'Let's go and see,' said Alex.

Turning on their torches they went outside.

They were just in time to see a fox going through their fence to the neighbour's garden. They heard hens clucking and so they rushed over to the fence and roared out loud! The fox dropped a hen and then quickly scampered away.

Lights went on in the house, and Mr Hazel came out. 'What are you two doing in my garden at this time of night?' he said.

They explained, and Mr Hazel was very grateful. He said, 'Thank you very much,' and gave them a bag of marshmallows and then called their parents to tell them of their adventures with the fox.

'Well done,' said Mummy.

'And you can go camping whenever you like,' said Daddy.

They had fun that night, cooking the marshmallows. They were hot, delicious, soft and crunchy.

Sam Khan-Mcintyre

Belinda Button In London

Belinda Button is a toy rabbit about two inches high. She wears a pink ribbon on her left ear and has always wanted to be an actress.

One day she decided she would go to London. She heard someone say that they were visiting London, so she jumped in the open pocket of their bag. She went on a big train and it wasn't very long before she was in London.

When she got to London she saw her old friend, Elliott the mouse. He offered to show her around. They went to all the famous places, Big Ben, the London Eye, the Tower of London.

Then, she saw a gold ring on the floor. 'What's that?' she asked.

'Hang on, I think I recognise it. It belongs to an actress. She won't sing without that ring,' said Elliott.

'Oh dear! We have to get it to her,' said Belinda. The pair then raced through the streets as quickly as they could until they came to a big theatre.

In the distance, they heard the clock strike seven. 'Hurry!' Elliott cried. They ran through a small hole in the wall, and made their way to the actress' dressing room.

'This is her room,' Elliott said.

Belinda struggled into the ring, wearing it around her waist and climbed onto the dressing table.

The actress was very pleased when she saw it. 'Oh, there it is!' she said. She put the ring on, and went on stage. Belinda hid in the wings and watched her, knowing she had helped after her wonderful day in London.

Amy Sellman-Bartlett

Three Little Bunnies

Berwick, Boyd and Benjamin scampered out into the road
They didn't stop to think about their highway code
Mother Martha clasped her hands in horror to her mouth
It was so very dark now, fast cars were travelling south
She'd warned her baby rabbits many times to take great care
But in a playful moment, they forgot that she was there
Then all at once the bunnies froze in the headlights of a car
Together they crouched in fright with little mouths ajar
Martha sprang into the road, she knew they couldn't run
She spread herself across them, with all three beneath her tum
She closed her eyes and lay as flat as she could possibly lay
And wondered would her babies ever see the light of day
Her heart was in her mouth now as the car sped overhead
And continued on its journey as down the road it fled
Benjamin stuck his head out and called the other two
Martha said with one eye shut, 'I'm very cross with you.'
She pushed them quickly off the road, into a field of hay
Where Berwick, Boyd and Benjamin, she knew could safely play.

Jackie Davies

Misha The Cat

In she slinks, her tail erect
And turns on her feline charm
Her proud back arches
And in sensuous elation
She rubs against my arm

What does she want? I ask myself
And why are cats so fickle?
She turns her whiskered face to mine
And begs me for a tickle

She starts to purr and sensually
Miaows and claws my legs
Without a doubt I know what's wrong
And give her the food she begs.

Susan J Roberts

Mr Pickle's Pet Shop

At Mr Pickle's pet shop the choice is quite extensive.
It's mystical and magical and not at all expensive.

Meet hairy dogs and scary dogs and one that yawns and yawns,
And playing in a nearby cage meet baby unicorns.
Meet fluffy cats and scruffy cats and one that's always smiling.
Descended from a Cheshire cat, she really is beguiling.

At Mr Pickle's pet shop the choice is quite extensive.
It's wacky, weird and wonderful and not at all expensive.

Sitting in a large top hat, magicians' rabbits wait.
One elegant white rabbit keeps insisting that he's late!
Meet brown rats, black rats and some you can't approach.
One claims a distant relative pulled Cinderella's coach.

At Mr Pickle's pet shop the choice is quite extensive.
It's awesome and amazing and it's not at all expensive.

Meet scowling owls and howling owls perched in a plastic tree.
There's one that winks at pussycats. He'd like to go to sea!
Meet blind mice, Miami mice and mice who have no tails.
They run and squeak, play hide-and-seek and terrify the quails.

At Mr Pickle's pet shop the choice is quite extensive.
It's curious, chaotic and it's not at all expensive.

Meet rare, red, romping dragons. No one's quite sure of their ages.
But Mr Pickle says they *must* be kept in fireproof cages.
Meet fruit bats, cute bats, a vampire bat called Guzzle.
But just in case he misbehaves, he has to wear a muzzle.

At Mr Pickle's pet shop the choice is quite extensive.
It's bold, bizarre and beautiful and not at all expensive.

Meet frogs who change to princes if they receive a kiss.
Meet friendly bugs who give you hugs - and snakes that simply hiss.
If you deserve a special pet to tell your secrets to, please visit Mr Pickle's shop . . . .
And say that I sent you.

At Mr Pickle's pet shop the choice is quite extensive.
It's fabulous and fanciful and not at all expensive.

Pat Simmons

Fruit Salad

'twould
be quite easy
to make poems
shaped as apples
round, symmetrical
mirrored halves
curved sides

or
pears
much
thinner
above then
swelling, out
and out and out
to be apple-like
at their base

and brown
kiwi fruit are
sort of square
and squat; but
of the lot the
simplest is a

green
grape's
shape.

Betty Don

Two Kids And A Witch

Once upon a time there was an old witch,
Who lived in a cottage, just past the third ditch.
With a mole on her chin,
And a mean, toothless grin.
The people of the village had lived in such fear,
None of them brave enough to ever go near.
A lovely new family of four,
Moved into the house next door.
Poor things completely unaware
Of the village's major scare.
The two kids ventured out to explore,
Not noticing the peeping eyes from next door.
With a glint in her eye, she beckoned them over,
Promising them ice cream, covered in clover.
The three of them decided to go for a walk,
And soon enough started to talk.
All of a sudden, oh what a pain!
The clouds turned grey and it started to rain.
The witch got frantic and started to fret:
'I can't get wet, I can't get wet!'
The kids looked round and were shocked at what they saw
The mean old hag was there no more,
They looked and called all around,
Nothing was left but a puddle on the ground.

And the rest of the village lived happily ever after.

Lara Birley

A Mouse Called 'Potty'

I know a mouse that's potty,
He climbs the festive tree,
And hangs down by his lengthy tail,
With a smile, for all to see.

He chats to the distant fairy,
At the very, very top,
Yet even though, she won't reply,
That does not make him stop.

He eats the candy walking sticks,
And blows out all the candles,
He winds up all the clockwork toys,
And hides in people's sandals.

He nibbles at the parcels,
In case there's cake inside,
And when, somebody's voice is heard,
He'll always run and hide.

He's very, very cheeky,
And wears a few disguises,
He borrows clothes from toy and bear,
In all sorts of shapes and sizes.

One day he'll be a soldier,
And then he'll be a ghost,
He looks very, very silly,
But it's the one I like the most.

So, if you hear some noises,
In the middle of the night,
Don't be afraid or startled,
Because it's Potty wearing white.

On Christmas morn, he's up at dawn,
Before we get a look in,
He wants to know what gifts we've got,
And if the breakfast's cooking.

I don't know why he does this,
As he only yearns for cheese,
And as we're having eggs and ham,
He will be hard to please.

This year is like no other,
As I dress for the day, I'll know,
That Potty will be in my shoe,

Where my foot's supposed to go.
But, although he's often trouble,
And a naughty mouse at that,
I'd miss his late night visits,
If we ever got a cat.

Hilary Ayling

The Fearsome Apple

There was an apple on a tree,
ripe, red and juicy,
he didn't want to be eaten,
afraid of the big sharp teeth,
he had seen in his dreams.
The sun was smiling onto him,
his brothers laughed and played,
autumn came with hungry children,
who picked all the apples away.
Trembling with fear our apple saw
those big white teeth with awe,
'Help, help, I don't want to die!'
but the teeth only tickled him,
so he started laughing
and laughed more and more
as he slid down the boy's throat
'Hey, that's fun!' he cried, getting thinner
and thinner,
swimming in the deep stomach pool,
what was left of him finally,
was pure vitamins,
travelling through the boys' veins;
Who said, 'Thank you! You gave me life,
my hunger is now satisfied!'
And the apple was proud
of the job he had done,
and laughed about his fear so loud,
the boy could hear his tummy rumble!

Sydney Krivenko

Count Gnatula The Vampire Gnat

I was sitting, lost in silence, looking down across the sea,
perched way up on a hilltop at Whitby Priory.
As I munched the crisps and sandwiches that I had brought with me,
a fearful, chilling shriek rang out. I jumped and spilt my tea.

Atop a wooden box I sat, beside a dry-stone wall,
with no one near for miles around, nobody at all.
So who had shrieked so close to me? Who was it, then, had called?
My wooden seat began to shake so much it made me fall.

The wooden top had lifted off, quite slowly, with a creak;
then nothing else. I craned my neck and shuffled close to peep.
From in the box - a frightening sight which left me very weak -
a cloakèd form stared up at me, with fangs and death-white cheek.

I couldn't move: stunned and numb, I was frozen to the spot.
The monster stirred; the air went chill though the day itself was hot.
He bared his fangs maliciously, I wondered what I'd got
with which I could defend myself. I hadn't got a lot.

Potato sticks and sandwiches against a vampire gnat?
A flask of tea? A lunch box? What's the good of that?
Then suddenly it dawned on me how I could lay him flat:
I gobbled up a sandwich laced with garlic cheese (low fat)

Garlic fumes I breathed into his face whilst I did toss
a whiffy sandwich at his head. He soon knew who was boss!
He cowered and cringed in fear, and then I fashioned out a cross
from a couple of potato sticks. Count Gnatula was lost.

Gnatula, the vampire gnat, whose bite meant death, for sure,
croaked, 'Fang, you very much indeed! You realise this means war!
- But not just now,' he added as he fainted to the floor.
Then he crawled back to his coffin and all was as before.

With haste, I filled my bag back up with sandwiches and cake,
praying that Count Gnatula would not yet re-awake.
Potato sticks and garlic did the job, but just you wait!
- Next time I'm in Whitby, I'll make sure I bring a stake!

Eileen Caiger Gray

Phillip Sweetdream

This is the story of Phillip the fairy
Who longed and dreamed to be big and scary

He wished to breathe fire like a ferocious beast
Instead he sprinkled fairy dust, the job he liked least

He wished his name was 'Buster the Mean'
But his mother named him Phillip, Phillip Sweetdream

He wanted to fly like a jet-fuelled rocket
But he had silver wings that could fit in his pocket

Phillip was tired of being a fairy
He wanted to be a tiger (but not quite as hairy)

He wanted to be a giant with enormous feet
And never eat vegetables, only meat

Or maybe a dragon with dirty great claws
And teeth like daggers in vice like jaws

Then Phillip sat down on his little toadstool
And thought, *was it really so bad being small*

A great hairy tiger, well he can't fly
He has no silver wings, not like I

A big-footed giant, he couldn't be quiet
And as for flying, well he'd have to diet

A sharp-toothed dragon couldn't sprinkle gold dust
If he breathed out fire it would turn to rust

Perhaps being a fairy wasn't so bad
Even though he was the only lad

And although his name was Phillip Sweetdream
He was the strongest little fairy I had never seen

Clare McAuley

Along The Verge

A bright red poppy
Blows in the breeze

A bright blue pheasant
Hides in the hedge

A tall white daisy
Salutes me as I pass

A bright-eyed squirrel
Darts across my path

A sweet little rabbit
Hastens from his habitat

A colourful fly
Alights upon my eye

And I make for home
Aware I'm not alone!

Barbara Tozer

Tom Was Late

Tom was late
For school one day
And he began to cry,
His grey pants had
A hole in the seat
And that was the reason why!

His teacher said
'Now don't you cry
We'll find another pair.
Now try these on
And wipe your tears
And the rest of you, don't stare!'

Marian Bythell

When Nog Met Spat

When Nog the dog met Spat the cat
It was such a terrible day
Their owners had made a bad mistake
For this they would surely pay

As they rushed from the house and into the car
They hadn't noticed the door ajar
Nog, when stirring from his sleep
Crept up to the door to have a peep

There in the corner, stretched out on his mat
Lay Nog's arch enemy, Spat the cat
Spat looked up with such a fright
He had never seen such scary sight

Nog's black shiny nose pushed up to the door
Nudging it open with his big furry paw
Nog's pointed white teeth, all ready to bite
But Spat wouldn't give up without a fight

He raced down the hall, Nog in pursuit
Down went the hall table and the bowl of fruit
Up the stairs, through the bedroom door
Skidded on the window ledge, vase now on the floor

Seeing his escape, Spat flew over the bed
Kicking Nog as he jumped over his head
But Nog, not wishing to be out done
Soon had Spat on the run

Into the linen cupboard, towels in the air
Then both tumbled back down the bedroom stairs
Panting heavily they charged through the rooms
Into the kitchen scattering the brooms

Spat jumped on the table, he felt safe there
Nog jumped after him, he didn't care
Dirty plates and glasses smashed onto the floor
A thousand pieces by the kitchen door

Then they looked back at the disarray
And worried about what their owners would say
They both curled up tight, sharing a bed
Planning to blame a burglar instead

Fiona Dedman

The Twilight Fairy Dance

'Twas twilight in the forest
And children all around,
Were sleeping tight in bed that night
And didn't hear a sound . . .
For on this summer's evening
Were all the little folk,
In merry prance, with song and dance
Beneath the large, brown oak.
A party for the fairies!
A meeting for the elves -
Who giggled loud in coloured crowds,
And chattered 'tween themselves.
The Fairy Queen sat smiling
Upon a soft pink rose,
'Midst little toots of fairy flutes
And pixie piccolos.
Flat mushrooms were the tables,
For seats were toadstools, red.
Their drink was supped from buttercups,
And plates were poppy heads.
The dance floor was a cushion
Of mossy velvet green,
The insect band played on a stand
Of chestnut shells and leaves.
The harp was strung by Spider,
His webs were used for strings,
Honey Bee hummed and Beetle drummed,
As Ladybird did sing.
The glow-worms lit the forest
As elven babes grew weak,
Pussy willow made a pillow
When they fell asleep.
And when the night was over -
When dawn broke through the clouds,
The wood was still, no noise could tell -
No sign of tiny crowds.
They'd left before the sunlight,
They'd scurried homeward bound,
Never seen by human being -
Hidden underground!

And there they stay 'til darkness,
But if you're out by chance,
Look carefully - you just might see
The Twilight Fairy Dance.

Lynda Ann Green

My Old Blanket

My old blanket! What can it do?
Anything you want it to!
Close your eyes and make a wish,
Shake it out. Flick and swish!

My old blanket! What can it be?
A flying carpet, wild and free.
Rising gently from the floor,
Hovering slowly towards the door.

My old blanket! What can it be?
A pirate island for Ted and me.
Stretch it out, smooth it flat.
Jump on quick - but mind the cat!

My old blanket! What can it make?
A fairy castle, and enchanted lake.
Kings and queens, wizards too.
Maybe a dragon and a goblin or two.

My old blanket! Have you seen?
It has made my mum a queen!
Together we dance in the hall,
Blanket, cloak, cat and all!

My old blanket! Yes that again!
But now it is a cosy den.
Pile some cushions, good and high,
Camping out beneath the sky.

My old blanket! Here with me,
Snuggled up around my knee.
Cosy and warm, safe in my bed,
Tomorrow's adventures dance in my head.

Rachel Canwell

Fanny Fusspot

Fanny Fusspot lived in a house,
In the village of Tinkum Tay
From the time she got up and till she went back to bed
She never had time for play.

She lived all alone in her smart little home
That shone like a clean new pin.
If a neighbour she saw she would chat at the door,
But seldom invite them in.

She worked very hard sweeping her yard
And keeping her lawn trim and neat.
She once had a cat, but she got rid of that,
Said she couldn't stand four dirty feet.

Although she was fussy and sometimes quite bossy,
She really was sweet and kind.
She got quite a kick helping old Mrs Flick,
Doing any odd jobs she could find.

Mrs Flick was her friend, who lived at the end
Of the road near the village green,
Fanny wouldn't take pay, 'It's enough,' she would say,
'To see your house shiny and clean.'

All around Tinkum Tay, Fanny dashed all the day,
Working hard helping folk here and there,
Cleaning windows and doors, doing all sorts of chores,
And doing them all with great care.

She collected the eggs for old Farmer Peggs,
And took them round to the store,
Then went to the dairy to help his wife Mary
When milking time round at four.

When the milking was done she would gaze at the sun
Setting low in the sky and would say,
'The work is all done and it has been such fun,
But I think now I'll call it a day.'

One day she called round to help Mrs Pound
Just like she had promised to do,
But her friend Mrs Pound just could not be found,
Mrs Flick's house was quite empty too.

She ran round to two other friends that she knew,
But neither of them answered her call.
Even down at the store it said 'closed' on the door,
Fanny could not understand it at all.

She went to the dairy but couldn't find Mary,
Nor could she find Farmer Peggs.
She let out a cry and said, 'My oh my!
How can I deliver the eggs?'

She set off home feeling lost and alone
When she could not find PC Tom Game.
Then she got quite a shock by the old village clock
When she heard someone calling her name.

She walked over to see just who it could be
But there was just no one in sight.
She set off once more but just then she saw
In the village hall there was a light.

She ran to the hall, taking care not to fall
And couldn't believe her eyes.
Inside the hall were her friends one and all,
And together they all yelled, 'Surprise!'

'Happy birthday to you, happy birthday to you,'
The village band started to play.
There was old Mrs Flick beating time with her stick,
Fanny just did not know what to say.

Mrs Pound looking grand went and took Fanny's hand
And leading her into the hall.
Said, 'It's your birthday and yet, we knew you'd forget
You're so busy helping us all.

You work hard all day, but never take pay
For all the things that you do.
So all Tinkum Tay got together to say,
'Fanny Fusspot today is for you'.'

David Henry Worsdale

Every Day God-Fairy

She is dancing, in the wind, as if one with the whole universe
She laughs at nature, and makes herself known to the world.

She is a hummingbird, a watchful eye she possesses.
All you need to know is to look at her, and see her long womanly fairy tresses,
and she will bless you during all your magical spells.

The God-Fairy is beauty, that surpasses all other fairies, and she is the vision we seek,
and need in our daily lives.

She makes husbands find wives and she moves like the breeze and makes the trees come to
life!
She is the fairy that takes hold of you and makes all beautiful dreams come true.

She is loveliness and serenity and peace lies within her fairy soul.
So let her take control and she will show you worlds and universes, you have never seen
before.

Adore her, and worship the God-Fairy and be as one with her in a time soon to come,
or the present or future and she will show you places you never been to before,
in another dimension . . .

the end . . .

Melanie Miller

Missing: Miss Peep, Bo

Monday 8am, I had just got to the office when the door opened and in came a flock of sheep all speaking at the same time.

'She's gone!'

'Not been fed yet!'

'It's dipping day!'

'She has my ribbon!'

'Is this the sweet shop?'

I fired my gun in the air and the bleating stopped as quickly as it had begun. I pushed my hat back on my head and narrowed my eyes taking in the scene.

Thirty white and woolly sheep filled the room, like a wall to wall carpet. I eyeballed the nearest grass eater and said, 'I'm Detective Inspector Wolf, now make like a hive and bee quiet, you, Lamb Chop, and who is missing?'

The sheep shrank before my gaze and in a small voice said, 'Miss Bo Beep Sir, she should have been at the paddock at seven o'clock, and she didn't show, what are we to do?'

I rose slowly to my feet and my stomach rumbled loudly, I had not had my Frosties yet but this was an open and shut case, I motioned for the woollies to gather closer and said, 'There could be several answers to your lost shepherdess, 1. She fell off a cliff. 2. She was eaten by a dragon. 3. Humpty-Dumpty fell on her, but I guess she forgot to put her clock back an hour last night.'

'Clock back,' said the sheep.

'Yes, Miss Peep just got off the bus, case solved.'

Bill Hayles

Uncle John-Paul

Quinn, Elliot, Torin, Toby and Amelie think they are fortunate children because they have a very special uncle. Uncle John-Paul was born with Down's Syndrome; he lives with Granny and Gramps in the country. Even though he can't do everything other grown-ups find easy, he is happy and kind, and never too busy to play games with the children. They love their uncle very much.

One day when the children were visiting Gramps, Granny and Uncle John-Paul, Mr Williamson, the next-door neighbour, called round, he was very upset because he couldn't find his cat, Spoodles.

Uncle John-Paul and the children went out to look for the cat. After a long search they found Spoodles caught up in brambles in a field. With the help of the children, Uncle John-Paul untangled the cat, getting rather scratched as he did so. He wrapped Spoodles in his coat so it couldn't run away, and they took it back to a delighted Mr Williamson.

Later that evening, while they were having tea, there was a knock on the door. Mr Williamson held out a bag, a 'thank you' present for finding Spoodles. Inside they were delighted to find a box of their favourite chocolates and the latest Dr Who DVD. Uncle John-Paul and the children are the biggest fans of the series. Rescuing Spoodles had given them all a warm snugly feeling inside, which was as enjoyable as the DVD and chocolates.

Rose-Mary Gower

The Sad Snowflake

Snowy was a beautiful, crisp white snowflake. But he was a sad snowflake. Why? I hear you ask. Because Snowy could make all his friends smile. But he couldn't make himself smile.

When Rainy the raindrop was sad because nobody was playing in his puddles, Snowy and his friend Icy the icicle made some multicoloured ice cubes to cheer Rainy up. Rainy smiled as he watched them melt into pretty puddles that everyone wanted to play in.

When Sunny the sunbeam was sad because everyone was too hot to work, Snowy sent out his cool friend Breezy to fill the stuffy offices with cool air. Sunny smiled as he saw everyone, now cool and refreshed, quickly finish their work and go home to sit in their sunny gardens.

When Cloudy the storm cloud was sad because everyone was looking at the sky wishing the storm would end, Snowy asked his friend Rainbow to appear. Cloudy smiled as everyone's grumpy faces quickly turned to smiley faces when they saw the beautiful colours in the sky.

However Snowy's friends all worried about Snowy because he never smiled. So they arranged a Smiley Meeting to plan what they could do. After much discussion they decided to collect all the Smiley Feelings they could find. Then they made them into a special Smiley Soup.

From that day onwards, whenever Snowy feels sad, he sips his special soup and is filled full of warm, smiley feelings.

Rachel Marie Sutcliffe

Mama Blew A Kiss

Mama blew a kiss
It escaped through baby's door,
Danced down Pole Street,
To be seen no more.
Where was it going?
Mama didn't know!

It bounced along a window
Landed on a roof,
Slid down the drainpipe
Then kissed a bulldog's tooth.

It greeted Mr Postman
And dived into his sack,
Sat upon an envelope
Pouted lips and smack!

It smiled at Ted the milkman
With teeth that shone like silk,
Opened up a semi-skimmed
Then kissed down all the milk.

It laughed at the paperboy
Throwing papers down the street,
Spotted a photo of the Queen
And kissed her on the cheek.

It sang with the local cats
Under the moonlight,
'Do you want a kiss?' it asked
And gave the cats a fright!

And just before midnight struck
It returned from whence it came,
Hovered over baby's cot
And kissed her once again.

Elayne Ogbeta

Little Henrietta

Little Henrietta
Comes clucking for some food
If she doesn't get it straight away
She gets quite rude.

She pecks on my window
With her very sharp beak
And when I go to feed her
She almost tries to speak

So I 'cluck, cluck' back to her
We cause quite a commotion
She knows I'm not a chicken
At least, I think she has a notion

When she's eaten all her food
She's off again for sure
But when the sun is going to bed
She's back again for more

And you will never ever guess
Where Henrietta sleeps
No, you'll never ever guess
To watch her is a treat

She sits on a wooden log
And takes off like a Jumbo Jet
She flaps her wings and flies to bed
She's never failed yet

I wonder if you can guess
Where Henrietta nests
She sleeps in an old tree
And safely has a rest

And there she sleeps till morning
And she opens her beady eyes
And then I hear her clucking
And her funny little cries

Now I know that little chickens
Are not supposed to fly
But little Henrietta does
And I don't know why

Chris Hoskins

Fred And The Monster
(For my two smelly little monsters)

Alone in a cave for 2000 years,
Slept a large green monster, with socks in his ears.

His snores were louder than a big steam train,
And they shook the ground like a landing plane.

Then one day, he started to wake,
As he'd just had a dream about chocolate cake!

His stomach was hungry and had started to rumble,
So he tried to get up, but he started to stumble.

So with a great big stretch and a great big sigh,
He wiped the sleep out of his eye.

Then he stretched out his legs and wiggled his toes,
Ruffled his hair and scratched at his nose.

He started to wonder how long he'd been there,
As there really was a foul smell in the air!

He sniffed around trying to find the source,
But we all know it was him, of course!

He'd not had a bath for ever so long,
That he really had started to pong!

So he tried to get up and this time he did,
And he left the cave, where he'd once hid.

He wandered over to a small group of boys,
Who were all playing loudly with their favourite toys.

But they took one look at the big green sight,
And all ran away, with screams of fright!

'Oh please come back, don't run away!
I don't want to eat you, I just want to play!'

But one boy didn't run. No, he stood tall.
And he wasn't scared, no not at all!

'Now listen here monster, my name is Fred,
And you cannot eat me, it's the rules!' he said.

'Now first you need a bath, I think,
Because you really, really stink!'

Fred covered his nose with his thumb and his pinky,
As the big green monster was ever so stinky!

'Now follow me over to the nearby stream,
So we can get you sparkly clean.'

The smelly monster was happy to oblige,
So off they skipped side by side.

He jumped straight in and gave a shout,
Then he started to splash and jump about.

When he was all squeaky clean,
He jumped back out of the tiny stream.

'Now then Fred, can you bake?
'Cause what I need now is chocolate cake!'

'I've been dreaming of it for years and years,
And if I don't get it now I'll be in floods of tears!'

'Well we'll have to go and see my mum,
But we'd better be quick, come on let's run!'

So off they went to young Fred's house,
And Fred crept in as quiet as a mouse.

He found some cake on top of the table,
So he took it and ran, as fast as he was able.

The monster scoffed and chewed and slurped,
When the cake was gone, he let out a huge burp!

This made little Fred chuckle and laugh,
As they walked together along the path.

'I must go now Fred, back to the cave,
But please don't cry, try to be brave!'

They hugged and kissed and waved goodbye,
And off the monster went with a tear in his eye.

Now back to sleep for 2,000 years,
So he put the socks back into his ears,

And he settled down with a nice full belly,
All nice and clean, not at all smelly.

And very soon he started to snore,
So loudly he started to shake the floor.

So if you find a cave, don't go in!
'Cause a large green monster may lie within,

With socks in his ears and a nice full belly,
And yes he may be terribly smelly!

But if you are fearless, like little Fred,
You may choose to go inside instead.

But if you do, remember to take,
A great big slice of chocolate cake!

Deborah Brownson

Noah And The Flood

Humanity appeared to grow so wicked
That the Lord, to cleanse the land
Decided to send a flood upon Earth
To kill all life with a wave of His hand.
Noah now 600, had remained steadfast
In his faith, a good righteous man
Blameless, without fault, God took pity on him
Saved his family Shem, Japheth and Ham.
Noah was ordered to build an ark
Of wood, to be three decks high
With tar to waterproof, stability to float
And compartments for animals to lie.
Noah had found favour in the eyes of the Lord
So all his family went into the ark
Pairs of every conceivable creature
It took days, and then it went dark.
The rains came down for 40 days
And nights, the landscape was nil
The waters covered the mountains so high
Now protected, the family was still.
150 days the waters went down
A dove was sent to find land
It came back to the ark with a leaf in its beak
On Mount Ararat the ark it did stand.

Catherine M Armstrong

Worm Friends

My sister and me always take it in turns,
To look in the garden for wriggly worms.
We found a fat worm inside an old shoe,
And decided to call him Wiggly-Woo.

We thought Wiggly-Woo would like a worm friend,
So we started to look around every bend.
We searched high and low and looked under trees,
And found a big worm hiding under some leaves.

My sister said, 'He looks all alone,
I'm picking him up and I'm taking him home.'
So we put him together with Wiggly-Woo
And decided to call him Diggly-Doo.

Then off we went to look for some more.
When our brother shouted, as he came through the door.
'Why don't you two listen? You will never learn,
You can't give homes to all of the worms!'

We looked at each other and both of us said,
'We will just keep these two, and collect snails instead.'
So off we went and we started to look,
In every cranny and every nook.

We looked inside flowerpots and under a pail,
To try and find a few little snails.
The sun went in and it started to rain,
So we had to stop till the sun shone again.

Our brother said, 'Haven't you looked long enough?
Let's have a pet that we could all share and love.'
'We would love a pet rabbit,' said my sister and me.
'Do you really think our mum would agree?'

We would look after him and clean out his hutch.
We hope Mum says yes, we would love one so much.
So we all asked our mum and she said she'd agree,
If we promised to be good and let the worms free.

So we all said, 'Goodbye,' to Wiggly-Woo
And set him free with Diggly-Doo.
So if you look hard when you search on the ground,
You might spot two worm friends wriggling around.

Patricia Lay

What Can I Smell?

I'm alone in the house, there's nothing to do
Dad's gone to work and Mum's got the flu
It's pouring with rain and there is nothing on telly
It's the first day of the holidays and I'm fed up already
I will play on my own and make up some new games
Putting animal noises to animal names

There's an animal in the house, what could it be?
Shall I look, shall I see?
There's a moo from upstairs, that shouldn't be there
What animal says moo?
Shall I look, shall I see?
It's not in the bathroom having a bath
There's just the cat in the window all covered in hair
'Do you say moo?'
'Miaow,' said the cat, so it can't be you

There's a cow in my bedroom playing with toys
Is it you who's been making this mooing noise?
'Moo,' said the cow
'You shouldn't be here, you belong on the farm
Now get out of the house to where you belong'

There's an animal in the house, what could it be?
Shall I look, shall I see?
There's a baa from downstairs, it shouldn't be there
What animal goes baa?
Shall I look, shall I see?

It's not in the kitchen, there's just Mum's new dress
I hope this baa doesn't make too much mess
The dog's in the hall but he doesn't baa
He just barks loudly at people and cars
There's a sheep in the living room on my settee
Drinking my milk and watching TV
'Do you go baa?'
'Baa,' said the sheep
'You shouldn't be here, you belong in a field
Now get out of my house, and take the milk with you'

There's an animal in the house, what can it be?
Shall I look, shall I see?
There's a bad smell from somewhere, it shouldn't be there
What animal could cause such a bad odour?
Shall I look, shall I see?

I think it's downstairs, it really does smell
But where it's coming from I cannot tell
The cat's with me now, he gives me a sniff
I hope he doesn't think I've caused this whiff
By the cupboard under the stairs the smell's very strong
I'll open the door and see what it is pongs
There's a huge pink pig curled up in a ball
There's mud in the cupboard and all over the hall
Is it you who smells?
The pig shook his head and covered me in poo
It is you who smells and now I smell too

'You have made such a mess, not to mention this smell
I am really beginning to feel very unwell
The sty on the farm is the place you should be
Not in the cupboard causing trouble for me'

There's an animal outside, what can it be?
Shall I look, shall I see?
It's shouting Robbie, that's my name
What animal says Robbie?
Shall I look, shall I see?

I open the door and look up the path
And see my dad pulling faces and making me laugh
Sorry I'm late, I've had a hard day
Cutting corn and baling the hay
Some animals went missing, but they are back now
A smelly old pig, a sheep and a cow.

Sean Hale

The Lonely Fish

Way down deep at the bottom of the ocean
There lived a little fish,
Who lived upon his lonesome.
He dreamed of a social life.
He longed for some friends.
If only he had a fishy wife on whom he could depend.

This can't be all there is, he thought,
There must be more than this,
I'll go and have a look about,
Thought the lonely little fish.

So off he went that little fish,
Excited but unsure.
'I can hardly wait,' he said to himself,
As he swam further up shore.

'I wonder who I'll meet?
I wonder what they'll say,
I wonder if I'll even find my fishy friend today.'

So on he went that little fish,
Determined to succeed,
Determined he would find some other fishy folk in need.

By now the little fish had swam a very long way,
In fact he hadn't realised but he'd been swimming all that day.
So feeling rather tired,
The little fish thought it best,
To settle down for just a while,
And take a little rest.

After just a little while the little fish awoke,
He had a dream of playing cards with another fishy bloke.
If only this were true, he thought,
I'd love a fishy friend.
It's lonely being on your own,
And I'm sick of let's pretend.

So feeling rather sad,
The little fish swam for home,
But what he hadn't realised was he wasn't on his own.

For miles she had been following and he hadn't even seen,
A pretty little lady fish who'd been where he had been.

She lived all alone at the bottom of the ocean,
She too did not enjoy her life upon her lonesome.
So feeling rather brave,
She swam up close beside him,
And in her sexiest fishy voice said,
'Hi, my name is Madeleine.'

Could he still be dreaming, thought this little fish,
Could this really be in front of me my pretty lady fish?
So trying not to blush, the little fish said hi.
To think he'd nearly missed her
And almost swam on by.

So off they swam together,
Two lonely little fish,
At last they had been granted their all time favourite wish.

And now they live together,
In love and in the ocean.
But now they have each other,
No longer on their lonesome.

Mia Brittain

No Chocolate For Sam

'Mum! I'm not well,
I don't know what's wrong!
My nose has turned red
And I'm all in a dwam!'

'I have a sore tummy
Although chocolate might help.
Do you think I could try some
Before it all melts?'

'No fever or shivers, Sam,
I think you're all right.
No chocolate for you,
Not even one bite!'

'But Mum, I'm not right
I could faint any minute,
A slither of chocolate
Could help me to shake it.'

'No chocolate!' says Mum
'Now get ready for school.'
Sam shuffles away
Trying hard not to drool.

Sam went to school
And dreamt of chocolate all day
He longed for the bell to ring
Lunch was hours away.

At last the bell rang
Sam shot out of his seat
He was very excited
And ready to eat!

Sam opened his lunch box
With almighty dread
He peaked inside it,
Not more jam and bread!

But to his surprise
On top of his lunch
Lay a huge chocolate cookie
For Sam to munch.

Sam gobbled it up
Crunch, crunch, crunch
His smile said it all
What a fantastic lunch!

Thanks Mum!

Sarah Broadley

Aunt Summer Rose

Home cooked fancies
filled with jam.
Shining teapot, sugar
topped basin.
A delicious teatime treat
for kids, and neighbours calling by.

Talk and chatter
of the nattering
down the road knowalls,
hold all brains
of untold secrets . . .
saying rain's about,
we need a fall.

We still await
our special guest.
Aunt Rose do hurry
you're the best.
You're like the tiny
furry field mouse.
Come to visit,
come to our house.

Sally Plumb

Suki's Seaside Holiday

Suki, the Border Collie, lay with head resting on her front paws in the corner of the sitting room. Her big brown eyes stared at the suitcase standing side by side in the middle of the floor. Each time one of the family came in she lifted up her head and looked at them as if to ask, 'Where are you going?' and, 'Can I come too?'

Soon Daddy came into the room and started to carry out the cases to the red car parked by the garage at the side of the house. Suki suddenly sprang to life, yelping and running round in an excited manner, wagging her bushy tail, fearful that she was going to be left behind. She did not have to worry for Mummy shouted from beside the car, 'Come along, Suki, good girl.'

Soon the panting dog was lying in her usual place under the dashboard in front of the passenger seat. The family climbed into the car and away they drove to their holiday cottage at Rockpool-on-Sea.

The little cottage stood on a hillside, overlooking a wide sandy bay. From the cottage a winding lane ran down to the promenade which skirted the golden sand.

Shortly after they arrived Daddy took Suki for a walk along the beach, whilst Mummy and little Karen went shopping in the pretty seaside town.

As soon as Suki saw the sea lapping the sand she ran off and jumped into the shallow waves. Then she stood there waiting for Daddy to play her favourite game. Suki liked Daddy to throw pebbles into the sea so that she could swim to the spot and dip her head under the salty water. The clever dog would then grab the pebble in her teeth and bring it back to the beach.

They played for about half an hour then Daddy called Suki to him and dried her with a big towel, which was Suki's very own.

When they got back to the cottage Mummy had prepared a lovely tea of buttered scones with strawberries and cream. Suki had a bowl of her favourite doggy food and then trotted off to her kennel in the garden to have a little sleep and dream about diving for pebbles.

One day Suki and the family went for a drive to Winkle Cove. It was a very hot day and, whilst Daddy, Mummy and little Karen were sunbathing, Suki was enjoying herself rolling about on the grassy slopes above the pebbly beach. She snapped at the flies that buzzed around her nose and then she chased butterflies that flew close to her. When Suki had tired of chasing about the grass she trotted back to where the family were sitting in their deckchairs. Little Karen was licking a big round sugary lollipop with a cat's face on it. Suki went up to her and began to beg for a taste but the little girl would not give her any. The big yellow sun got hotter and hotter. This made little Karen fall asleep. The big lollipop dropped from her hand, onto the pebbles and the naughty Suki picked it up in her mouth and ran off to a grassy bank, where she soon gobbled up the sticky sweet.

When little Karen awoke she began to cry for her missing lollipop but neither Mummy or Daddy knew what had become of it. Daddy called out to Suki who was lying on the grassy bank and when she ran up to him he saw the lollipop stick stuck to her hairy coat. He scolded the naughty dog and promised little Karen another lollipop on the way home.

Terence Leslie Iceton

Ray, The Rainbow Trout

There was once a beautiful fish called Ray. He had the most beautiful scales in many colours and was called a rainbow trout. He was extremely proud as he had seen himself in a broken mirror that had been thrown in the river. It was hard to understand at first when he noticed his reflection as he thought it was a friend but due to his intelligence he concluded that the shiny mirror showed a picture of himself. So he grew to understand how beautiful and shimmery he was.

He was a healthy fish and loved to lash his tail and dart around in the wonderful world of the river. There were so many underwater plants and interesting fish and he longed to know all about them. He had a beautiful big mouth, too, and loved to send bubbles out to pop on the surface of the river. His scales shone with such colours, silver, pink, blue, purple, turquoise, that was why the humans called him a rainbow trout.

However, Ray was not perfect because two weeks ago he had nearly been eaten by a pike. Pikes are fish too, but are big and even have teeth and Nasher pike thought Ray would be a nice lunch. Nasher took one big snap and got him in his teeth. Ray struggled for his life and managed to wriggle free but from that day he had two deep wounds on his back. The wounds were not fatal and he began to get better but forever he would have two ugly scars.

When he felt well again he forgot about his terrible scars, but everyone else could see them. He loved to dart off and meet other fish and make friends but some of the fish were so unkind and rejected him because he was not as beautiful as them. 'Ugh,' some of them said, 'what's wrong with you? Go away.'

Poor Ray became so unhappy that they did not like him and want to be his friend. He smiled at them with his beautiful mouth but they said unkind words. How cruel of those creatures. Ray became more and more unhappy because he needed friends.

Then one day he was caught on a fisherman's line. Instead of letting him die, the fisherman put him in a bucket of water and took him home for his pond. His two children were so excited and took it in turns to feed Ray every day. They never even noticed his scars until the sun shone on them one day. 'How did it happen?' asked the children.

'He must have been bitten by a pike,' said the father. Ray was happy to be looked after by the children. He thought he was a good present for them and thrashed about the pond whenever they came. Each day he made them laugh and smile as he was like a ray of sunshine dancing and flashing on a rainy day.

Mary Braithwaite

Fairy Story With Smiles

A tiny angel, or yet a fairy, she typed this one out
Danced across my keyboard here, this I've got no doubt
As I sat a watching, wondering was she struck dumb?
Yet in amazement as I sat her little feet amazingly spun

Hopping, skipping, dancing, she tapped this out to you
Tapping at my keyboard here, yes dear children it's true
Glancing at the screen to see was she talking to me
A smile upon my face, disbelief at what I did see

Smile you, will you smile, your face is always glum
I daily sit on your shoulder, you're the one looking dumb
Good grief she could read my mind, my mouth was now ajar
All the children need to smile right across the world so far

Possibly some won't believe, assume you typed this out
But if it makes them smile then there's room for doubt
As a fairy I'll touch each heart just a short brief while
Hence all are reading along here, everyone wearing a smile?

No, I'm not struck dumb I'm hoarse, shouting at you all day
Giving you inspiration, the sweetest things yet to relay
For every doubting Thomas, I'll leave you a ten-inch nose
Then they'll all believe this fairy story, magically as it flows.

Christopher Robin Slater

Family

Percy's mother loved to dance
She enjoyed a jig, how she could prance
Stately and graceful she danced to the beat
For such a stout pig she was light on her feet.

She taught her daughters, how to stand
On their hind legs alone, they looked very grand.
They learnt how to waltz, and a reel or two,
Said Percy, 'That's something I'd never do.'

Meanwhile the farmer's boy watched and muttered,
Under his breath he quietly stuttered,
'They are just a lot of pigs,' said he,
'Me father thinks more of them than me.'

Percy was happy out in the yard
Till the boy found a stick and beat him hard.
He chased young Percival into a corner
Shouting, 'Now who looks like little Jack Horner.'

Percival's father surveyed the scene
Un-noticed by boy and pig he'd been
He summoned his family saying, 'That's enough,
This lad is getting far too rough.'

In a circle they chased the boy round and round
Till he stumbled and fell with his nose on the ground.
They emptied the water butt all over him
Whilst Farmer George smiled and no longer looked grim.

Diana Blench

The Poet's Story

A handsome poet strolls the night by the riverbank,
Looking at the indigo and cyan stars as they glow.
Suddenly, he waves to the crimson moon,
Dreaming to climb up to visit it soon.

An owl speaks to him from a willow tree,
It tells him that the moon has a surprise for him -
A pretty princess is waiting for him on the moon,
Because she wants to marry someone to be her prince.

The young poet says to the owl,
'I am not a prince, all I do is write poems!'
The owl tells the poet to send a poem to the princess,
Because she will love to hear the music of poetry.

The poet wonders how the owl knows this,
But he is afraid to ask this friendly owl.
Suddenly, the owl says he is her messenger from the amber moon,
And this is how it knows she will love to wed him.

Tri Tran

Spell

There isn't an *a* in sentence,
And effect as a noun has none,
And the plural of woman is women,
A lot is two words not one.

Definite has no *a* either,
And thank you is two words, you see,
And it's only when it's is short for it is
That it has that apostrophe!

I'm sure you can make up your own poem
Of words you get wrong all the time.
You just have to remember it's easier
To put all the rules into rhyme.

Fran Harris

The Red Rocks

We play on the red rocks
Hide-and-seek
And climbed like monkeys
And looked at the sky

Beside our house
We walked in wildflowers
And played like bees

All those years ago
When I was young
And I hope children today
Will remember just like me

Happily ever after
Is what I say
I am still a child
Because I still remember
The red rocks
And the dancing bees

Kenneth Mood

My Pet Sister

I'd like to have a goldfish
I'd like to have a cat
I'd even like a hamster
And I wouldn't mind a bat
A puppy or a guinea pig
And definitely a rat
I just don't want a baby sister
Drat, drat, drat

Kathy Charvin

My Love

When I met you I was young
Torn apart and full of sadness
You healed the hurt in me
Made my life complete
We had a family
Two lovely children, you agree
Together we grew strong
Forgot about the past.

I loved you so my love
I lived for you my love
Summer days were long my love
Days of joy
Still I cried for you my love
I would have died for you my love
Our summer nights were long my love
Just filled with joy.

You've suffered so my love
And my heart has broken
To see you struggle on
Through pain and woe
But the treasure in our hearts
And the music in our souls
Will see us through it all
Together we are strong.

I love you so my love
I live for you my love
Our autumn days have come my love
These days of joy
I'll comfort you my love
Take your pain away my love
In my arms you're safe my love
Rest your head my love.

You know I've said lots of things to you
But the truest words to you
Were when I vowed my heart
And pledged my life
Fifty years have swiftly passed
And in gold our love is cast
I will love you all my life
And through eternity.

I will love you so my love
I will live for you my love
These autumn hues of gold my love
These days of joy
Just take my hand my love
Take my life, my heart, my all
These autumn nights are sweet my love
Safe and full of joy
Safe and full of love.

Olivia Gribble

Dreamtime

As I floated through the cosmic mists
Over an angry turbulent sea
I espied a strip-ed tiger fish
Being landed on the quay.
I then saw a zebra crossing
And a pelican followed suit,
I met an owl with laryngitis
Who couldn't give a hoot.

A chocolate covered penguin
Lay melting in the sun,
A hyena started laughing
Was it really having fun?
Did all this really happen
In this place I love to be?
Of course, and plenty more besides
It was my dreamtime, don't you see?

Loyd David Burt

O Majesty

O Majesty, your mighty hand,
Will see us safe within your land,
The rivers running to be free,
What beauty for our eyes to see.

The grass so green, so lush 'tis food,
For animals that you made good,
The tall trees - in the woodlands grow.
It's work for men you made it so.

You made the stars, that shine so bright,
The moon to guide us in the night,
The gentle breeze that rock the waves,
To you we sing our songs of praise,

O Majesty, your mighty hand,
Will lead us to your promised land,
So let all Heaven and Earth rejoice,
For we will hear your mighty voice,
And when all things have come to pass,
The victory is yours at last.

Mary Turner

The Little Acorn

Once upon a time, in a faraway field,
Stood a large proud oak, an acorn it did yield.
It bounced on the ground, and then rolled away,
Asleep over winter, there it did lay.
Waiting for spring, and the sun to glow,
Just like his dad, he is waiting to grow.
Tall, strong and proud, the view he'll command,
To inherit his kingdom of all the woodland.
For now he is sleeping, through the winter severe,
Awaiting his moment as it's getting near.
So if you see an oak tree with a little acorn,
You'll see something special, a king soon to be born.

Anthony David Beardsley

My Grandma

My grandma is so nice to me,
She is pot full of thrills.
She knows many ways to please,
Telling fairy tales is one of her skills.

She listens to me patiently;
To my feelings she shows care.
If my mum is busy to play with me,
My grandma is always there.

She stitches me warm sweaters
And she is always busy cooking.
She fills my bag with treats
When my mum isn't looking.

She takes me to familiar places,
And to places I have not seen.
Once we went to London,
Where we saw our Queen.

She buys me the things I need,
And everything my heart desires.
She gets me whatever I ask for,
Her love for me never tires.

She looks for my merits
And never the mistakes I make.
How could I do without Grandma?
Who would bake me a fruitcake?

When I become old and my turn comes,
I will try not to whine.
But be an adorable grandma,
Just like this grandma of mine.

U S Jaiswal

Old Foxy

Old Foxy was alert as he went on the prowl
Dinner he did crave especially if it was fowl
He knew where he was going, a farm lay to the East
Nothing could stop him from reaching his feast

He sniffed at the air with pleasure so immense
He had reached his destination but was stopped by a fence
His annoyance was quite clear as he stared in disbelief
So near, yet so far, this problem caused him such grief

Thinking how to overcome this barrier to his meal
He nudged the fence with his nose so an opening he might feel
His frustration overwhelming, his determination grew
So many hens in the coop, he wanted just a few

With excitement he eventually found a hole in the fence
Now from him the chickens would have no defence
Barging through the hole, he slinked along the ground
He was expert at this, he didn't make a sound

But the hens were not fooled they were wise to his scent
Clucking with fear, the alarm up to the farmer went
Old Foxy was almost upon them, his eyes wide with greed
Right there in front of him was his nightly feed

The hens, feathers flying, ran in panic to and fro
But Foxy had his orders, three chickens to go
He was about to pounce when the farmer fired his gun
Old Foxy didn't stop he was having too much fun

Another shot rang out, this one was very near
Foxy dropped his precious prey as he trembled with fear
His only thought was to get away, he ran with all his might
And he didn't stop running 'til the farmer was out of sight

Barbara Lambie

Fairy Dreams

While I was in my garden, from the corner of my eye
I thought there was a fairy, I looked again, just a butterfly
I told my friend what I'd seen, to hear how she would feel
She said that I imagined it and fairies were not real

I looked and searched for many days, no fairies could I find
I sat and sobbed upon the grass, when I heard a soft voice, so kind
A pretty bubble floated by, it glistened with rainbows in the sun
Magical and colourful, I jumped up and began to run

I chased the bubble to the flowers at the end of my garden
There the bubble burst into a shower of glitter, fairy dust and then
A fairy smiled and waved to me, on the buttercups, she stood
I gazed in wonder, joy and glee, as she fluttered as a fairy could

'My name is Willow, I live not far,' then she pressed into my hand
'A fairy wish, a rainbow star for safety in dreamland.'
I gazed down upon the star, the magic glowed so true
When I looked up she was gone, just the dancing bells so blue

Although Willow had just vanished, I knew I could be glad
I'd seen her just as I had wished, I'd never now be sad
I held the star in my hand, her secret I can keep
In the pretty flowers, where I stand, I know that she might peep

When I went to bed that night, I thought of Fairy Willow
I knew she'd keep the promise, I put the star beneath my pillow
So I closed my eyes to fall asleep and thought of what I'd seen
That night I dreamt only the sweetest of sweet dreams

So, for the happiest dreams, just remember Fairy Willow
And know that believing in fairies puts magic under your pillow!

Catherine Howarth

Norman The Naughty Baby

Baby Norman was always naughty. He would get into his mam's make-up drawer and write on the walls with her favourite lipstick. He would play in the mud then roll around in a pile of clean clothes that were ready to be ironed. Naughty Norman's parents would tell him, if he didn't stop being naughty Santa wouldn't leave him any presents. But naughty Norman didn't care.

Naughty Norman would refuse to eat any of his dinner but would steal from his Dad's plate. He would put worms in his sister's shoes. His parents would tell him, if he didn't stop being naughty Santa wouldn't leave him any presents. But naughty Norman didn't care, until …

Christmas Day came. Santa left only coal in his stocking, no presents. He watched his sister unwrap her dolls and costumes and other amazing toys. Naughty Norman snatched a doll from his sister.

'Norman don't be naughty,' his mam told him.

'Santa brought you coal because you were so naughty,' said his Dad.

'Here Norman.' His sister handed him her shiny new ball. 'You can play with this if you promise to be good all year.'

Baby Norman nodded and kept the promise even though it was very, very hard.

When next Christmas came Norman didn't have coal in his stocking but lots and lots of presents.

Norman the naughty baby was naughty no more.

Laura Alderson

Lost For Words

One: I got lost. Two: The police were called. Three: I was shouted at - for doing what I've been told not to do.

I'm often told what not to do. And I'm often shouted at. If I wasn't shouted at I'd probably not do the things I'm told not to do. It's not complicated! But adults seem to think it is. And that's a problem. Adults complicate things that are simple. Whereas things like friends and fashion - things that are complicated - well we all know what adults think of them.

Mum and Dad are adults. Long Tall Barry and Short Fat Sally. That's what they call each other. They think it's funny. Mum says she calls Dad that because of an old rock 'n' roll song. Dad says he calls Mum that because of her size. It's strange though because she isn't short or fat - she's tall. Not very tall, just taller than most. And she's old. Not very old, just older than everybody else's mum. And it's Dad that wears the heels! They get on very well, Mum and Dad. They like the same things - just differently.

Anyway, getting back to the story. The police came and I got shouted at by the adults for getting lost - something I obviously didn't do on purpose. Duh!

And now I'm upstairs writing about it. Which just goes to show - it was worth getting lost after all. All writers have to suffer for their art.

Robin Cowpertwait

The Swing

It stood on the lawn
Waiting so still
A board and two ropes
Sturdy pillars, until

A small child with a lolly
Came bouncing from bed
Dressed in pyjamas
With curls on her head.

Unbrushed, unwashed
Bedraggled with sleep,
But awake, full of life
And ready to leap

On the swing, it moved with a jerk
Down drops the lolly
On to the earth.

All else is forgotten,
Swing, swing, swing, swing
Lucy shut both her eyes
And began to sing

'I'm happy, so happy
My birthday is here,
I'm happy, so happy
My treat is the fair
That comes every year
On the green.'

The swing boat's name is 'Happily Ever After'
And belongs to a giant
As big as a bear,
But I never see him
He's left me his swing
As a present from him every year.

Rhoda Hazelden

My Bedroom

There's something in my bedroom
It runs off with my toys
I look but I can't find it
You see it makes no noise
But I know he is in there
Because I've lost my things
All the very small bits
That my mother brings
He hides them in a dark place
Just under my bed
'You should put your stuff away lad'
That's what my mother said
But when my room was painted
Mum found all of my stuff
All dirty on the carpet
And covered in piles of fluff
'Where is the thing that takes them?'
I asked as she turned round
'No one takes your stuff love
You just drop it on the ground
We did find Sammy Spider
But he will do no harm
I sucked him up the Hoover
So do not be alarmed
Your room is nice and clean now
No creatures left in there
So when you go to bed tonight
You'll sleep without a care.'

Jennifer Melbourne

Flissy

Hello, my name is Flissy and I am a butterfly! I grew from a chrysalis, which is a sort of shell. I remember the day I first opened my eyes and looked around to see my beautiful wings, which were now starting to tingle! Because now they wanted to fly!

I had four wings and the colours were amazing! They were bright orange and black with a little bit of red, and I am called a Red Admiral.

Now I need to stand up on my wobbly legs but they seem to be stuck! I have six legs, which seems a lot somehow to 'unstick', so I begin to clean them with my long tongue and this seems to do the job nicely. At last I am now up on my feet and my wings are flapping ready to fly. So here I go!

It is wonderful up here looking down on everything below. Oh what is that? It is very big and black and white and is making a strange noise like a *moooo* sound! 'Oops sorry, I seem to have landed on your nose,' I say to the creature, that has now crossed its eyes.

'Oh that is alright, it happens all the time,' said the creature.

'What are you?' I asked.

'I am a cow and my name is Daisy,' it replied.

'I am a butterfly with no name, can you give me a pretty name too?' I asked.

'Yes, I shall name you Flissy.'

Andrea Trick

Happily Ever After

It's 9 o'clock on a Monday morning, again! Mothers and fathers bringing their young toddlers to nursery, pushing, shouting and shoving. The children pile into a tight classroom lining up for the awaiting teacher. The children, push quietly, pour into the empty room, sitting down patiently the children wait for the teacher's entrance.

Leaping, skipping and jumping, bouncing up and down from side to side waving her arms and legs through the air around her. The children are gobsmacked, 'Good morning,' she yells happily. 'We're going to do some keep fit,' she exclaimed, her voice screamed. The teacher then starts bouncing round all four corners of the room with star jumps, the children sit motionless, wondering where this new burst of energy has come from. 'Come on kids, what are you waiting for?' she enquired, at a yell once more.

Throughout the half hour lesson the teacher continues to display herself at top speed round the room, the children remaining motionless, press-ups, sit-ups, running on the spot, weight-lifting unused desks and side bends.

Where did all her energy come from? This is a weird lesson! all the children think to themselves in confusion.

The end of the lesson the teacher quickly runs to the front from the back, grabs hold of the piece of chalk and writes down, 'Well, there was no lesson plan today so I thought I'd give you a little show!' Whilst writing this down yelling it at the same time, her voice excited for some reason!

The children, throughout the lesson had no idea what to do, no idea where to look and no idea what to say or do. Their bums were glued to the seat, as they say. Bums on seats as the old thespians used to say.

At the end of the day, what a burst of energy the children had! As they were tucked into bed that night, 'Never again will I ever miss school!'

And their parents lived happily ever after!

Gary Thompson

The Best Way To Spend Your Holidays - Kids

The lake at Codnor, resting
by the old coach road.
The pleasure of the locals
is apparent by their attendance mode.

The van where lots of people get their breakfast cobs;
and the fishermen have long since filled the keep nets,
showing off their latest reel and fishing rods.
The gear they bring! Is absolutely everything.

For hours they sit and wait with
baited hook and bread to allure
the tench and perch, they are very small,
in fact, they're not worth fishing for at all.

The dads are proud to show their kids
the way to fish and dig
for worms to supplement the maggot tin,
or the brand new flask he brought the whiskey in.

A two man tent they pitch,
and if the weather holds they will stay the night and fish.
'Hey! Shhh, be quiet, I think I've got a bite,
ask Fred at peg 52 to bring his biggest keep net to this site . . . '
As if . . .

Kathleen Bartholomew

Adventures

Sometimes when I lie snug in bed
All kinds of thoughts drift round my head.
Exciting tales we read in class
Run through my mind, and then I pass
Into a story's magic world,
Through mad adventures I am whirled.
Exploring a huge distant star,
Driving a Formula racing car.
Leading a polar expedition,
Playing a tennis exhibition.
A cowboy on a covered wagon,
A knight on quest to slay a dragon.
A gladiator bold in Ancient Rome,
A shipwrecked sailor far from home.
An Indian chief with eagle feather,
A prisoner running through the heather.
A star ship captain lost in space
Menaced by an alien race.

Imagination ranging free,
All of these people I can be.
And when it's time to say goodnight
Adventures always turn out right.
I love this world locked in my head
When I lie dreaming in my bed.

Don Nixon

He's Not My Dad Any More

My dad used to play football with me on Saturday mornings.
Now he stands on the sideline, shivering and cold.
He cheers when I score a goal,
But he glances at his watch, wanting to go home.
He is not my dad any more.

My dad had sparkling eyes and thick black hair.
My mum was always telling him to get his hair cut.
Now he has no hair at all.
It all fell out because of this medicine he has to take.
He is bald. His eyes look big and tired.

My dad was always laughing.
He went to the pub for a drink with his mates
And when he came home he talked too loud and Mum complained.
He doesn't go out much now.
His voice sounds like it struggles to work.

My dad and me, we went for long walks together.
We took turns to throw a ball to the dog.
We looked for conkers and scuffed through fallen leaves.
Now my dad can't walk very far at all.
Mum pushes him in a wheelchair.

My dad did healthy things like swimming
And gardening and riding a bike.
Sometimes he went to the gym. He was wicked fit.
Now his medicine makes him sick and some days
He can't get out of bed.

He's not my dad any more.
I loved my old dad.
I love this new dad more.

Jean Cullop

Who Did That?

I sit then scratch then fall on my back
Ouch! That hurt,
Whack! Who did that?
I slowly climb as I watch out for another attack.

Who's creeping about on the stairs?
It's making the hairs on my neck pop out.

I'll pounce, I'll jump, I'll grow like two bears
Miaow! I declare, 'Go away, go away!' I shout
'Can't a cat sleep on the stairs?'

As the sun falls my tormentor does go
I wonder where?
I'll never know!

Paul Harkin

Jethrine And Pearl

Two little kittens full of mischief,
playing hide-and-seek
in the garden, amongst the flowers.
Bees, butterflies, ladybirds
can be found around them.
Seeing a bee on a flower
Jethrine wriggles her tail
and pounces.
Pearl sees her disappear
then hears her sister's cry
Running to the voice
Pearl sees Jethrine
all wet in the birdbath
squinting.

Jessica Stephanie Powell

Little Glue Boy

There once was a boy,
He was made out of glue,
He stuck to all things,
Just like gum on a shoe.

He was so embarrassed,
As in public he stood out,
Everyone would laugh,
And some people would shout.

'It's not bad to be odd,'
His mum had said,
'It's good to be different,
So enjoy it instead.'

But no matter how,
Hard he tried,
The bullies would bully,
And make him cry.

So when he was twelve,
He decided to leave,
He got to the door,
But got stuck to his keys.

He walked on for miles,
Until he reached the sea,
And in the distance was a girl,
With things stuck to her sleeves.

He realised right then,
She was made out of glue,
So they kissed on the lips,
And made one out of two.

Hannah-Lea Coyne

The Angry Crocodile

I am an angry crocodile
I love to hunt for food.
Please join me for lunch
As I'm always in the mood.
Although I'm not fussy
Some things I will not eat.
But most things I'll devour
Especially if it's meat.
If you wish to join me
Look within my pool.
Put your head under the water
And give my name a call.
Then I will come to greet you
And take you out to lunch.
We'll roll along together
Until your bones go crunch!

Steve Eastwood

Billy

Look there is movement in the dark,
With yellow eyes that seem to spark,
What can it be that lives out there?
It appears to be covered in fur,
Has black as black as coal,
Fearing nothing for it is bold,
It makes not a sound,
As it walks over the ground,
Slipping past all,
Into the hall,
It always comes to our call,
Why it is Billy our cat,
And we all are glad to see him back.

Pauline Uprichard

Araminta

Araminta Higginbottom had a big name for a small girl. She loved ice cream and was always first in line. But the other children got served before her, because the ice cream man couldn't see her.

Araminta loved pushing the supermarket trolley. But Mum always put things in the wrong trolley, because she could not see Araminta.

Her favourite treat was football on a Saturday, but she could only see the match from Dad's shoulders.

When Grandad took her to the circus, Araminta was spellbound by the trapeze artists. She applauded when the tamer put his head in the lion's mouth. But she was wide-eyed when she saw an extraordinary unusually tall clown. After the show Grandad took her to meet him. The clown showed Araminta how to walk on stilts and Grandad bought her some the next day.

When she heard the ice cream van, Araminta put on her stilts and toppled out. But the ice cream man couldn't reach to pass her the cone.

On the way to the supermarket, Mum couldn't keep up with Araminta. When she got there, Araminta had already demolished a pyramid of tinned beans and two shelves of cereals!

On Saturday, Araminta put on her football scarf and stilts. She looked forward to seeing every goal. When Dad pushed through the turnstile, Araminta tried to follow, but the stilts got tangled in the gate and she missed the match while she was rescued by firemen.

Araminta said, 'What's so great about being tall?'

Kim Russell

Living Dolls!

Sarah and Lucy were playing in their new playhouse and the sun was streaming through the glass windows. Lucy took her old doll and threw it into her pushchair and started to laugh. 'Don't be so cruel Lucy; you wouldn't like it if the doll did that to you!' Lucy laughed out loud.

They stepped into the garden and in front of them was a large pink and yellow doll's house! They cautiously approached it and pushed open the pink front door. Inside they were amazed to find tables and chairs with napkins, knives, forks and spoons all neatly arranged. Suddenly the door burst open and standing in front of them were two adult-sized female dolls, dressed in polka-dot dresses, wearing plastic shoes and blonde wigs. They gazed at the two newcomers with much surprise!

'You're just what we have been praying for,' said the taller of the two. 'We need someone to do the cooking and cleaning.'

Sarah was 10 and was used to doing some housework stared at her younger sister who was just 8 years old in horror! *Am I having a nightmare?* she thought to herself.

'You've been sent here because you have been horrid to our smaller cousins,' shouted the smaller of the two dolls. 'It's your punishment for being so cruel!'

Sarah and Lucy ran out of the doll's house into the garden and entered the playhouse. Lucy cuddled her doll and carefully placed it in her pushchair.

Denis Mayes

Learners All

The path ended by the lake's edge. There was still early morning mist in the air. Peter shivered in the chill. He could smell something strange. The smell seemed to linger on the high, long grass. What on earth could it be? Then he heard a crunching noise. He drew closer to the sound.

Suddenly, right in front of him, was a big dog fox. It was chewing on a rabbit it had caught earlier. Peter did not like that. As a boy of only ten he hated this side of life. He liked bunny rabbits, like to see them with white tails bobbing up and down.

He knew now the funny small noise was that of Reynard, the fox. He waited a while and then heard another noise. Out from behind an old tree tumbled three small fox cubs. They were playing at catching rabbits in the grass. Several young bunnies were scampering around in danger. Then came a loud thumping noise on a patch of bare ground. A warning. Immediately the bunnies scattered and ran for their burrows. Supervising the retreat was a very large adult rabbit, their leader. The fox cubs were no match for him and they turned tail and ran back to their parent who was still chewing away. They decided to join in and pinch a few titbits. This made the big fox angry and he cuffed them smartly. Chastised, they gave up for the day.

The little bunnies had survived thanks to the thumper. The question is, for how long would they avoid the foxes? Their burrows provided a temporary safe shelter but Thumper would not always be there. They needed to be careful always.

Peter felt pleased the bunnies had escaped and went home.

Elizabeth Stanley-Mallett

Bath Time

The boys looked at the house, it was three storeys, white stucco walls, statues in the landscaped gardens and a fountain. Corthan, the instigator of this adventure, looked over at Gawyne and whispered, 'See I told you there wouldn't be any trouble.'

'Thorban won't like this,' said Gawyne.

'Only if we are caught my friend, and I don't plan on telling him.' Corthan looked pointedly at Gawyne. He nodded his head in resignation. They proceeded stealthily across the garden using the shadows and as much cover as they could find.

They found the correct basement window very quickly and with some fine manipulation by Corthan, using a piece of wire purloined from their guardian, they opened the window and entered the basement. Unlike the basement at their home, which was just stone and earth, this one was clad in fine woods and carpeted. The walls were adorned with paintings and in pride of place the aforementioned hot tub. The boys started to strip down in preparation for getting into the water when they realised they weren't alone. From the corner of the room strode a figure, it took them moments before they realised that the figure was little more than clothes, no hands, no feet or head were visible. The boys shouted in alarm and in a rush ran from the room, leaping from the window then sprinting as fast as they could go from the house and grounds. The figure placed towels on the edge of the hot tub …

Eric Lyon-Taylor

Confused And Young Life Embraced Within Fear

I recoiled, tense into my chair, fraught with fright,
As a furious storm unleashed all of its might,
Every clap of thunder making the walls vibrate,
Every lightning flash, brighter than dawn doth awake,

Torrential rain pounding upon shelter of roof,
Became a copious waterfall descending on earth,
As it gushed to ground forming meandering streams,
Seeking babbling brooks for its severity to appease,

The thunderous storm was awakening my inner fears,
Whence a ray of delight in the doorway did appear,
Gliding in a baby walker with more grace than a swan,
Arms stretched out for solace, from her anxious alarm,

I cradled her in my arms and wiped away the tears,
For the heavenly wrath was her first encounter with such fear,
Yet confusion in her face spoke more decibels than the storm,
As her soft hands squeezed my nape I could only weep forlorn,

Perplexity reigned . . . wherein my own confusion dwells,
How to comfort purity from birth . . . of what's my stormy hell,
So I caressed her with tenderness to pacify infant mind,
Yet she lovingly kissed my cheek, as a please don't cry . . .

Surely life hath no more beauty than a child within arms,
But it also holds more terrors that we cannot pre-foretell,
Yet when the confused and young life embraced their fears,
They conquered a storm's depth, whence their fears disappeared . . .

Barry Pankhurst

A Magical Grandmother

There was a very bad storm outside.
A little girl sat up in bed,
And she cried.
She was afraid of the thunderstorm.
She prayed for an earthly angel who would keep her warm.
Before she knew it,
Her prayer had come true.
Her grandmother came in and said,
'I am here for you.'
She stroked the child's hair,
And kissed her forehead.
And on the soft cushion,
This little girl rested her head.
Outside her window,
She could now see the moon.
He smiled down on her.
She knew she would sleep soon.
Not long after that,
She could see the stars, too.
Her grandmother said,
'Those are my gifts to you.'
A grandmother's kiss,
It melted away the storm.
A grandmother's love,
It kept the little girl warm.

Laraine Smith

Friendship

I don't need friends from
The upper crust
I just need friends
That I can trust
Love and friendship
Can turn to dust
Like faded photos
Or cars that rust

Your name can be Russell,
Elsie or Jack
Your skin can be yellow,
Blue, green or black
You can wear market trainers
Or an old brown sack
Just don't call me tramp
Behind my back

If you are a person
Who just won't share
Or a callous soul
Who just doesn't care
Or even a bully
Who can't play fair
Look for other friends
There's plenty out there

If friendship could be bought
In shops that sell flowers
Or chocolate log cabins
With greeting card towers
Then the rich would be joyful
The lonely all poor
And my very best friend
Would never knock on my door

For I'd rather have one friend
That's caring and funny
Than ten false friends
With hatfuls of money

David Dooley

When I Grow Up

I shall have a whole bar of chocolate
to myself. Fry's chocolate cream I think.
And I shall get up late and never eat sprouts.

I will drink only red pop and Coca-Cola
and jump up and down on the bed
and swing on Grandma's washing line.

I am going to walk on every wall I come across
and tell old grumpy Jones next door to shut up.
I am going to win a noble prize in some competition.

I shall slush through mounds of leaves and jump
in all the puddles and get my wellies wet inside
and I shall stay up late and play as long as I want.

I will grow tall and dark and handsome
and have a cloak and a stick with a bird's head
and possibly wear a hat on special occasions.

When I am even more grown up I shall go away
and be a doctor and do good things for Africans
and support my mother. And possibly my brother.

I will buy myself a gold watch.
I shall probably never marry.

Chris Raetschus

Spaceships

Spaceships are cool
Spaceships are very fast
Spaceships' jets are very hot, hot, hot
But you always, always, always, always, always
Bring your dried space food
Because it makes you hungry in space
Travelling around this very big place.

Paddy Smith (9)

My Garden Alphabet

A for apple, it's blossom so fair
B for bluebell with sweet dainty air
C for crocus, says spring's here again
D for daisy, makes lovely long chain
E for erica on heathland and moor
F for fuchsia, in pot by the door
G for gentian in deep shade of blue
H for holly, has red berries too
I for iris, such tall flags to see
J for jasmine, makes nice scented tea
K for kerria in fine shade of yellow
L for lavender, its sweet scent so mellow
M for marigold, like old English ballad
N for nasturtium, just add to a salad
O for orchid, exotic with grace
P for pansy, has cute little face
Q for quince, nice jam can be made
R for rose, which never will fade
S for sunflower, so tall, strong and bold
T for thrift, could this mean some gold?
U for ursina, will close petals at night
V for violets, a lovely spring sight
W for wisteria, a sweet climbing shrub
X for xanthoceras, too tall for a tub
Y for yucca with cream bell-shaped flowers
Z for zinnea, loves sunshine for hours.

Derrick Wooding

Happily Ever After

Many tales we all hear
A princess and her prince who sweeps her off her feet
Happily ever after can really be near . . .

Two horrible stepsisters, one girl left to do chores
Pumpkin turns into a carriage; you won't have to clean floors
Best dress you have ever worn and shoes made of glass
Danced with the prince, left at midnight, dropped a slipper, tries it on you, fits just right

A runaway with black hair
Creatures adore her, they all sing in tune
Hiding in a house with seven small men but that nasty witch in disguise offers you an apple
Lay deep asleep awaiting a magical kiss

Visitor stays in a large house
The owner stands by a flower wanting to break a spell
With not even a sign of a little brown mouse
House objects talk
In the end you will break the spell

Many more tales, maybe untold
A woman pricks her finger on a sewing machine, asleep for a thousand years
A young woman half-human, half-fish, becomes a human
Sultan's daughter flies away on a mat, he may not be rich but he is her prince
A woman falls in love with a man of another culture fights for her happily ever after
A woman disguised as a man to save her father, found out by her prince.

Many tales we all hear
A princess and her prince who sweeps her off her feet
Happily ever after can really be near . . .

Lucy Ann Smith (15)

Fairy School

It was yet another day at St Michael's School, where the cool fool and rule.
However on this day, there was a new teacher on his first day, called Mr Davies. The children
of the class smiled, before they each took their turn to introduce themselves. 'Hi, my name is
Simon, and I like to read a book,' and they all took a good look. There was Nicola, who liked to
dance, given half a chance - Ralph, who liked to wriggle like a worm, although it made Amanda
squirm and Sarah who liked her dolls and to take them on her hols.

'Well, I like tennis, have a wife and two children,' Mr Davies said. 'Now why don't you
type something about me,' he added. Susan typed, 'Mr Davies has brown hair'. However
she wasn't aware, as she was sitting on her chair, that the teacher had started to change. He
started to feel very strange; his hair had turned bright blue! As to why, he didn't have a clue!
Rebecca wrote that he had funny ears; Mr Davies hadn't felt so strange in years! Suddenly
he'd grown horns on his head! Then Amanda typed that he had a beard; it was just as he had
feared; Mr Davies started to feel weird, over her laptop Amanda peered - his beard had turned
long and white, like Santa Claus! He'd even grown bear's paws! Mr Davies was suddenly
wearing pyjamas - the children in class laughed - was he going bananas?

Colette Breeze

The Giraffe And The Insect

On a hot day when the sun was beating down, the smell of grass was heavenly. A giraffe stood beneath a very tall tree and ate the leaves from the top.

At the base of the tree was an ugly little insect. It had crawled out from underneath a brick. The giraffe stooped his neck down and inspected the little insect.

'Where have you come from?' he asked.

The insect looked at the giraffe and said in a small voice, 'I live under this brick.'

'I see,' said the giraffe.

'I have come out to play in the sunshine,' the little insect said. 'I am rather hot.'

The giraffe reached up to the top of the tree and bit off a succulent leaf. He bent his neck again and gave the leaf to the little insect.

'Here, take this. It is really refreshing and tastes good.'

The little insect thanked him and crawled on to the leaf and began to nibble at it.

'It really is very tasty,' he said. 'Thank you very much.'

'My pleasure,' said the giraffe and loped off into the bush. He felt really pleased with himself. He had done his good deed for the day.

Anne Mullender

The Wren

No robin sang his sonnets that day,
The blackbirds were out of tune,
The clouds raced over the stormy bay,
In that bleak and fateful June.

A little wren had died that night,
He loved to sing to the jay;
When he didn't stir in the morning light,
His friends gathered around to pray.

Around his little feathery nest,
They sang like a heavenly choir.
Then they laid him down to rest,
And mourned him on a sacred spire.

Sydney Wragg

Winter Wind

Rattling all the windows, tugging at the thatch,
Rampaging around the house, can't quite lift the latch.
Whistling through the soffits, luring us outside,
But it's cosy here indoors, by the fireside.

Munching buttered crumpets, quaffing cocoa too,
So bluster yourself inside out, make hullabaloo!
Rage through apple orchard, shake and split the boughs,
Swirl the leaves in vortices, round and round the house.

Raise ructious commotion, vent pernicious spite,
Dash the ships upon the rocks, douse the watchman's light;
Whirl the sails of windmills, topple teetering trucks.
Drag the legs from under the trestle viaducts.

Transplant our old toolshed, uproot warning signs.
Crash computer systems by downing power lines.
Do your worst, you tempest, because, when you're done,
With a myriad bursting buds spring will have begun.

Tony Newman

Three Million Two Hundred Years And Two Weeks Ago

(For the littlefolk)

Last night I was told a story and I want you all to know
About a dinosaur and his family, it happened many long years ago
The dinosaur was grazing by a swamp, lazily chewing his cud
Looking down past some trees into the misty bubbling mud

The dinosaur was happy and little did he fear
Suddenly from that swamp some bubbles did appear
As he watched from that swamp, it bubbled madly and then
First there was one, before he knew it there was ten

Those bubbles moved together, suddenly they became just one
That dinosaur shook his head and looked up at the morning sun
Now from that swamp, more and more bubbles did appear
Again they moved together like he had seen in the past
Lazily chewing a branch from a tree, knowing this would not last

But thousands of bubbles did appear and now they moved to ground
As that dinosaur looked he did find, hundreds more were all around
As he looked the sun began to rise, the large bubbles shed their skin
How was that dinosaur to know, mankind was to begin?
He looked at the far and distant sea and there he saw many, many more

Suddenly there was more and more bubbles, coming fast to the distant shore
The dinosaur looked at his family, he gazed at them with pride
How was that dinosaur to know, that more bubbles would be coming in with each tide?
Now the bubbles had shapes and some even moved into a small huddle

Those new creatures were now drinking from a large new puddle
Oh how was that poor dinosaur to know, that Man's time had begun?
That dinosaur began to laugh, he knew he would not be here for long
For those bubbles, now dancing, could it be? They are singing an Irish song

Yes, that is the story I was told as I lay sick in my bed
It is the story true of Ireland and that is what my grandad has just said

F K McGarry

Will They Understand?

Will the children of tomorrow
know the pain and the sorrow
of living in a bare and barren land?
Will they understand? Will they understand?

Will they see a different scene
where grass is brown instead of green
and all the rivers have turned to sand?
Will they understand? Will they understand?

Will they look and wonder why
there's no birds up in the sky,
all we've left is a barren land.
Will they understand? Will they understand?

Will they ever find a solution
to our poison and pollution
when they're living in a barren land?
Will they understand? Will they understand?

John Simons

Be Cool At School
(For Caitlin)

When your homework gets too tough
and you get down and stressed
put it down and walk away
have five minutes' rest

If it's still too tough when you return
don't get in a strop
take it with you into school
let the teacher do their job

They're there to help and guide you
not just punish and tell off
they're really not great ogres
sizing up children to scoff

So when in class if you are stuck
you need a helping hand
just raise yours into the air
and say, 'I do not understand.'

Trudi Collis

My Cupboard

My cupboard isn't big,
But not too small,
It isn't too empty,
Yet it isn't too full,
My clothes hang in it,
From ceiling to floor,
Bits still fall out,
When you open the door,
I wake in the morning,
Time to get dressed,
I like my clothes neat,
All ironed and pressed,
I look in the mirror,
Ten times a day,
To check myself out,
So I look okay,
I close its grand doors,
And jam it shut,
My cupboard keeps growing,
It's time for a cut!

Jennifer Brogan

Christmas Fairies

'Are there such things as fairies?'
Mary asked her teddy bear.
'Do they visit while I'm sleeping
and rest on my bedroom chair?

Do they dance each night with elves
whilst I'm in the land of dreams
and are they the ones to blame
for Mum's missing custard creams?'

No words did her teddy utter
because perhaps he didn't know
but outside Mary's window
tiny footprints glistened in the snow.

Bob Sharp

My Princess Kerrie

I tried to think of things to say
Don't worry, don't fret, you'll be OK
I tried to think of things to say
Don't worry . . . I love you; you'll be OK
I tried to think of things to say
It's nothing . . . I love you; you'll be OK
So I hold her, kiss her; it will be OK
I tried to think of things to say
Now all I can do is sit and pray
I tried to think of things to say
Dear Lord . . . make my princess be OK
I tried to think of things to say
Now I wait, a minute, an hour . . . a day
I tried to think of things to say
But all I can do . . . is hope and pray
I tried to think of things to say
No matter princess, whatever they say
I love you; and I'm there . . . for the rest of our days

(This true story has a happy ending
The threat of cancer has gone away
Peter wed his princess Kerrie
To live happily ever after from this day)

Peter Goldsmith

Hope Springs

There, dangling from the fallen tree
A pair of denimmed legs swung near
The forest floor. A silken knee
Criss-crossed its twin, demurely clear.

The boy's right foot tipped up and down
On nervous automatic spring;
The girl's beneath a summer gown
Uncrossed and gave a gentle swing.

At length the four together closed,
Caressed; in new embraces met.
What legs had hid was now exposed,
A record time may yet forget.

Cut deeply in the ancient bark
Brought out by lichen in relief
Beneath an old high water mark
A heart told still of love's belief.

A wrinkled leaf, a tad afraid,
Lay trembling in the dappled glade.

Godfrey Ackers

Paul Dickie

My name is Paul Dickie
They say I'm quite thickie
But I am as wise as an owl
For a flannel and soap
Will wash dirt off a dope
But you can't wipe a smile off with a towel

A cat hates a dog
Wood makes a log
And night ends in the morning
But if night never comes
Someone has not done his sums
For how can a new day be dawning

If water was dry
There would be no tears to cry
And no rivers to run to the sea
No need for a bath
Now that makes you laugh
But what would you use to make tea

You can draw a picture in blue
The breath inside you
You can even draw a curtain
You can draw on a straw, draw on a bridge
But you can't draw on a pin, that's certain

Terry White

Santa's Reindeer

Did you ever wonder how Santa's reindeer got their name?
Well, listen carefully and I'll tell you how they came to fame.

Now Dasher is the oldest, he always loves to run,
Kicking up his hooves is how he has his fun.

Dancer is as graceful as the beautiful falling snow,
She seemed to float everywhere no matter where she'd go.

Prancer is always one for acting like a dill,
She was prancing since time began and no doubt prancing still.

Now Vixen is one who makes every reindeer sigh,
For they always seemed to fall over themselves whenever she walks by.

Lady that's what Donna does mean,
and it seems to suit her just fine, or so it would seem.

For the boys there's Comet and Blitzen, twins from Heaven by and by,
How they got their names is easy, they were born from a crystal sky.

Then there's Cupid, the most shy of them all,
But when you're around him you can't help but in love fall.

So now there's just one left, the most famous of Santa's call,
The one they call Rudolph, the biggest riddle of them all,
For his name means nothing but he doesn't have one regret,
For his name is the hardest, the hardest to forget.

And now my friend you know the tale of how the reindeer got their name,
But, shh, remember, keep it a secret for after all, it's part of their game.

Natalia Small

Rain: God's Emotions

It's raining!
The Lord is elated,
Heaven's decorated,
Celebrations!
Upon His servants,
Showering His blessings,
Music, the wind's creating,
Trees dancing to melody,
Pure innocence, no felony.
It's no dream, but true story,
Oh Lord! I bow to Thy glory.

It's raining!
The Lord is unhappy.
Sky's gloomy.
Silence!
Depression engulfs us all,
As conscience gives a call.
We plundered God's every gift,
Entire humanity is on a drift.

It's raining!
The Lord is angry.
Hell's fury
Chaos!
Humans crying,
Animals dying.
Winds add to woes,
And trees shed tears.
As the pain grows.
Apologies O Creator!
Give us a chance to lead life better . . .

Akshay Chougaonkar

Sky Jam

Santa Claus was on his sleigh,
delivering gifts for Christmas Day.
As he flew through the cold night sky
he was dreaming of a hot mince pie,
so he didn't see the witch's broom
until he heard a tremendous *zoom!*
'Take care, you fool,' the old witch shrieked.
She swerved away. The broom shook and creaked,
then it spun right round with an angry roar
and crashed into an aeroplane's door.
The plane braked hard and a flock of birds
cawed, 'What's going on? It's too absurd!'

Then a second plane came the other way
and stopped to ask, 'What's this delay?'
More witches flew to join the crowd
and Santa shouted, very loud,
'I must get on, my sleigh is packed
with presents, in these bulky sacks.
I cannot let the children down -
please let me pass!' The witches frowned.
'There's too much traffic now,' they said.
'This can't go on.' They shook their heads.
'The sky's so busy here at night -
perhaps we need some traffic lights.'

They waved their wands and lights appeared,
and everybody clapped and cheered
as colours changed, red, amber, green,
the best lights that they'd ever seen.
Then everyone went on their way,
the witches, planes and Santa's sleigh.
Though night-time skies are still quite crammed,
there are no more lengthy traffic jams!

Sue Smith

My Pet Henry

I have a pet called Henry - he's the best one I've had yet
He's not a cat, he's not a dog and no one's met him yet
I think my Aunty M will probably scream
When I take him on a visit - I don't think she'll be keen
He's a very good companion and he doesn't smell at all
He isn't very big and he's really not too hairy
I think my Aunty M will find him pretty scary
He's been on shopping trips - although I've not told Mum
Occasionally I've shared with him a piece of pink iced bun
He sometimes is quite naughty - he's clearly not a saint
I think my Aunty M will probably faint
But the day has finally come, to introduce to her
My newest little pet - who definitely won't purr
I'll take him down the stairs and wait for a reaction
My Aunty M's response will cause me satisfaction
Because I know she'll scream and scream and get her coat and hat
Because you see young Henry is a real live hooded rat
I thought I might in future get a pet that's really vile
A prehistoric scaly-backed and dangerous crocodile
I can put him in the bath so Dad will get a fright
It would be really scary if I put him there at night
But I might be given a dog, or even Aunty's cat
So I think I'll stick to Henry, my sensational hooded rat

Margaret Whitehead

The Meeting

The witches had a meeting today
They held it in my house
I saw them start arriving
One was dressed as a mouse.

I could not hear what was said
Not where I was sat
One arrived a few minutes late
She looked just like my cat.

Where oh where will it all end?
I asked but got no reply
Then with a buzz and a flapping of wings
The chairman arrived, dressed like a fly.

The meeting lasted quite some time
Then suddenly it was over
It seemed to be a great success
And the tail quickly wagged on my dog Rover.

The witches now began to leave
And I slowly raised my hat
But the one who came as a mouse forgot
And left my house as a bat.

I hope they meet again quite soon
I enjoy having them here
Then I'll invite all of my friends
And show them there's nothing to fear.

Barry L J Winters

Tim Grows Fins

'Come on love,' said Mum holding Tim's hand tightly, 'the water is really warm.' Tim shivered and looked around at the other children enjoying themselves. All he had to do was walk down the steps into the blue water, but the bottom looked so far away! He had been so excited on the way here to their local swimming pool, remembering trying out his swimming actions in the bath at home and watching Jasper his goldfish swim round and round his bowl - he made it look so easy!

But since arriving, everything seemed bigger and noisier and what was that strange smell? Tim shivered even more so Mum took him over to where she left her bag and pulled out a towel which she wrapped around him, so at least he stopped shivering and felt warmer. 'I thought you wanted to swim like Jasper,' said Mum.

'I do,' replied Tim, 'but I feel sick.'

'What if you had fins like Jasper,' asked Mum, 'would that help?'

Of course, that's what he needed and he nodded his head. Mum reached into her bag again and brought out two bright orange things which she then blew up like balloons and placed one around each of Tim's arms. They felt strange at first but they certainly reminded him of Jasper. Then Mum pointed to some other children in the pool wearing them. 'Now,' said Mum, 'shall we have another try?' And this time Tim couldn't wait to get into the water.

Barbara Coward

Lobsters

Hamish took the lobsters out of his boat, one to keep for their supper, and the rest for the hotel. With the tourists coming to Tiree he could sell as many as he could catch. The spare pots he put back in the shed overlooking Salum Bay and locked the door. He then hauled his boat higher than usual for the time of year, above all the tides and overturned it on the grassy bank, protected from all sides but the sea. It was in its element with views of the sea.

He turned to his cottage and walked up the grass to it. He was ready for bed, even more than ever before in his seventy long years fishing, as if the chill he seemed to have caught meant business.

Cyclists coming to Salum via the grassy track from Modar twenty years later, park their bikes in view of the rotting boat. They sit on the grassy bank to view a Dun, which they will visit when the tide goes out.

'I wonder if the fisherman who left his boat with such care thought he'd never come back?' he said.

'Only in his dreams,' she replied.

'He's tucked her in so well,' he said, taking her hand.

Robert Shooter

The Rainbow Rose

Have you ever, ever seen
the rainbow rose?
It's very hard to find.

It doesn't live
in a flower bed
but only in the mind.

Do you dream, too,
about the rainbow rose,
this rose that blossoms at night?

And do you dream, too,
in colour or are your
dreams in black and white?

Maree Teychenné

Teddy Bears

Teddy bears new or old
Big ones, small ones
Brown ones, white ones
Grey ones, orange ones
Soft ones, hard ones
No matter what they are
They are all cuddly
Soft and loveable
So look after your teddy bears
As they never grow old

Ella Wright

Rupert The Toucan

Rupert the Toucan lived in the jungle, and much admired was he
his home was a nest two thirds the way up the jungle's highest tree.
A splendid bird was Rupert, all colours and plumage you see
and he was loved for his sense of humour and his generosity.

In his youth he was a carrier toucan, passing notes for generals of war
dodging bullets and bombs he flew with aplomb, still higher and higher he'd soar.
So great were his acts of wartime heroics, he was awarded a medal all clean
so he pruned his feathers and polished his bill, and went off to see the queen.

'So you must be Rupert,' her highness exclaimed. 'An honour to meet you indeed.'
'I present you with this cross of distinction,' for which Rupert was mighty pleased.

So home he flew with his medal all new and pinned tight to his chest
and after some days of flying so hard, Rupert spotted his nest.
The monkeys screamed and the cheetahs roared as they saw Rupert arrive.
They were so pleased to have their friend back and the hero still alive!

A party was held that's talked about still, amongst all of the jungle's old beings
there was cake of bamboo and plenty to chew and of course plenty of singing
And as he grew older Rupert would tell stories of battleships and how planes fell
to the kids of the jungle who all sat around, until their dinner bell would sound.

Rupert worked hard to gather the food, all berries and fruit to share
and critters would come from all over the place for feasts by the Hogwarts lair.
One night Rupert would not come from his nest, he said he was tired and needed the rest
his wings were stiff so he went off to sleep, to dream dreams only he could keep.

The creatures that gathered, though all very sad, just to have known him
felt terribly glad.
And a great party was held, imagine if you can
to match the great life of Rupert the toucan.

Tim Mason

Those Jumberly Bumberly Words

Those jumberly bumberly words I see
Dancing all over my page,
Well they just won't let me read them Miss
They're filling me with rage!

They won't keep still, they won't just sit
And let me read them well.
They just keep running amuck Miss!
What they say I just can't tell!

Those jumberly bumberly words I see
Are pulling funny faces!
I'm trying to read them clearly Miss
But they keep on switching places!

They won't behave, they won't just smile
And stay there in their place.
They move so far around my page
They might as well fly off to space!

Oh please Miss won't you tell them
'Settle down' or 'Nice sitting please'
So I can just get on with my work Miss
And read these words with ease!

Emma Caudwell

Childhood Fantasies

My sweetest souvenirs are my charming childhood fantasies
I still reminisce our lingering little fancies,
Indefinitely inscribed in my agile young memories
I am so fond of narrating my cheerful childhood stories!

My parents were my maiden words when I learned to talk
They instinctively inspired my slow steps till I could walk,
Each night before sleeping when I felt alone and afraid
Lovely lullabies and beautiful bedtime stories they eagerly read.

When I was so little, galore fascination and fun I had
With my tiny toys and playing with Mum and Dad,
My real role models, who tirelessly taught me how to read, write and pray
To love without prejudice, to learn and humbly obey.

I remember when I was five, how we used to chase cowardly grasshoppers
Me, my brothers, sisters and chums watching and waving at hurrying helicopters,
In the ageing afternoons play hide-and-seek till we tire the dying day,
Then do horrendous homework before Mum lets us watch TV anyway.

At ten, whenever we visited the countryside we trapped birds with small strands
I recall our inconceivable illusions that we could touch the sky with our bare hands!
Our grandpa's fanciful folklore full of myths and mysteries we curiously marvelled
Scary bush baby cries and tales of nightingales' sweet songs we revelled!

And though I open a new progressive page each dear day I live
My unageing fresh mementoes will indefatigably relive:
Like trivial thorns the oblivious negligible miseries
And like a blooming rose my charming childhood mischief, memories and mysteries!

Joseph Madedo

I Wish I Could Fly

Dad came with me to fly my kite;
we heard its lifting, flapping fight,
swirling, swooping into space,
dipping, diving, changing pace,
with each loop gaining greater height.

What fun I'd have in clouds so white,
with flowing tail, by string held tight,
climb like a kite, float, soar with grace,
feel safe with Dad below.

More magic still, I'd fly at night,
through darkness warmed by stars' soft light.
the skies would be a velvet place,
where I could stroke the moon's kind face;
then turn for home and be alright,
feel safe with Dad below.

Sally Carter

Play With Me

Mum can you play with me . . . ? Play with me . . . pleeassee . . .
Help me build a great *big* tower . . . then watch me pick you a flower . . .
Dad can you play with me . . . ? Play with me . . . pleeassee . . .
I will race you to the play dough . . . ready, steady, gooo . . .
Nanny can you play with me . . . ? Play with me . . . pleeassee . . .
Show me how to bake a cake . . . you always make it taste sooo great . . .
Grandad can you play with me . . . ? Play with me . . . pleeassee . . .
Help me build the very best train track . . . we can dress up and wear builders' hats . . .
Everyone can you play with me . . . ? Play with me . . . pleeassee . . .
We can all play a game together . . . before we have our tea.

Emily Jane Walters

Unexpected Hero

This chubby toad with half a nose,
had picked a fight with a thorny rose
The sight of blood had made him faint
and fall head first like a drop of paint

This toad was also rather old
and suffering from a frightful cold
His throat was sore, no croak escaped
eyes red raw and a head that ached

Alone he sat under silky leaves,
his ample tummy on his knees
This warty body began to wheeze,
frightening birds down from their trees

Other toads then gathered near,
but in a clearing, they had no fear
He'd warned them several times before,
but they thought him silly and such a bore.

Strange sounds were coming from a shed,
then rustling in a flower bed
Squelchy footsteps all around
A shadow cast on the muddy ground

This toad then mustered all its might
and sprang with ease, like a bird in flight
The human giant screamed and fell,
landing in a wishing well

Amazed to see this awesome sight,
the other toads then cheered all night
This toad was really not a fool
in fact he'd turned out to be cool

Angela Hoare

Fourth Of July Party

We've sent the word
To the whole of the jungle
You crazy creatures
Get ready to rumble

It's the fourth of July
And we're ready to swing
Get down and get sassy
Come and do your thing

Don't get snooty with me
You spotted faced cheetah
Get on the dance floor
And move those feetah

Hey Lion dude
Get outta your rut
Swing them shoulders
And jiggle that butt

Now Monkey man
Is a real mean swinger
He's a disco diva
And a beautiful singer

Hey there Snake
You piece of sly
Stop looking at Mouse
With your hungry eye

The hippos are swinging
They're treading that mud
They're looking like dancing
Is right in their blood

Rhino boy
You're doing the stomp
Whoa look out boys
He's ready to romp

Now I'm a bear that's rude
So show me to the food
I got funky hair
I don't care if you stare

Put some oil in my joints
You slippery oinks
This Giraffe can move

Just watch my groove

This Elephant ain't fat
You foolish Cat
But if I come down there
I'll squash you flat

Listen out for this Bird
I'm the best you ever heard
The drums are my dream
You can keep the tambourine

Come on now you guys
Get on the dance floor
Parade that hoof
And shift that paw

Elizabeth Crompton

Why I Am Super Special

I have got really ticklish toes
And a cute little button nose
I'm very tall from foot to head
And I get to sleep in a big kid bed

My hair is extra curly
And my feet are super twirly
It's too hard to stand on one spot
So I always run around a lot

But my most special thing of all
Is not my hair being curly
My feet being really twirly
My cute little button nose
Or my ticklish toes

My most special thing of all
Is that Daddy says I twinkle like the star above
And Mommy says I'm real easy to love
And that's why I'm so super special!

Kim Davies

The Fox And The Cat

Did you ever see the cat, with the feathers in her hat?
Not just any feathers mind, hers came from a duck's behind.
You see . . .
It gave the cat such pleasure, and was her greatest treasure
Until . . .
One winter's night after dark, Cat went hunting in the park
Looking for a tasty mouse, to take back to her cosy house
But a fox was watching her . . .
'Well hello pretty little cat, what a simply charming hat.

Poor Cat filled with terror
Shivered
And shuddered
Then shivered some more
Until her treasured feathers
Fell to the floor.
Cat bent down to pick them up
Just as Fox snapped jaws shut.

Fox had swallowed Cat . . .

But Cat didn't give up
No
No
No
No!

She hissed and kicked, clawed and spat
Then spat and clawed, kicked and hissed
And in the end
Fox was
Very
Very
Very
Sick!

Cat slipped out of the fox's throat
But she did not wait to gloat
She picked up her feathers
Disappeared among the heathers
And was never seen again

Did you ever see the cat, with the feathers in her hat?

Jennifer James

A Magic Carpet Ride

Last night I drifted to the other side,
On a beautiful magic carpet ride.
To a land where pixies and fairies play,
And vivid colours brighten each day.
I landed safely where the fairy tree stood,
Deep within some mystical wood.
And there below a blue marshmallow sky,
Perched upon a branch way up high.

A fairy queen with pure silken wings,
Reflecting the sun like golden sequins.
She beckoned me to cross over the stream,
Into a world of enchanted dreams.
Fairy dust hovered like silvery thread,
Floating and circled above my head.
Surrounding me in a kind of magical ring,
Then I noticed I'd grown two tiny wings.

A host of butterflies broke out in song,
A unicorn trotted merrily along.
A pure white swan hummed a lullaby sweet,
As I was swept right off my feet.
The spirit of happiness held out her hand,
Together we flew above the land.
Sweet freedom whispered into my ear,
'Come little bird, there is nothing to fear.'

The fairy queen nodded a big friendly smile,
As I settled beside her for a while.
She said, 'This is a fantasy, a magical show,
The purest childhood you'll ever know.
Cherish and keep it inside your heart folds,
For it all disappears once we grow old.
A journey through childhood precious like gold,
Where wishes and dreams are ours to behold.'

Then she pointed towards where the bluebirds whistle and fly,
Then sprinkled her moon dust, and bid me goodbye.

Sharon Cawthorne

Clichés Are As Common As Muck

Clichés are as common as muck; so don't *you* ever be stuck
On a cliché - oh no! That would be a shame, not just for your grades,
But because they are : overused, unimpressive, uninspired and clichéd!

Remember the rules!
1. Compare with the key words: 'like' and 'as' -
2. Clichéd: you've heard them before - *smart similes:* they are original, your own!

As thick as a brick	- As thick as *custard*
As sharp as a knife	- As sharp as a *point*
As plain as Jane	- As plain as a *maid*
As easy as pie	- As easy as *hopscotch*
As right as rain	- As right as the *heavens*
As thin as a rake	- As thin as a *cane*
As slow as a snail	- As slow as a *worm*
As good as gold	- As good as a *diamond*
As quiet as a mouse	- As quiet as *night*
As brave as a lion	- As brave as a *musketeer*
As short as a dwarf	- As short as a *midget*
As quick as a flash	- As quick as a *second*
As bold as brass	- As bold as *James Bond*
As loud as thunder	- As loud as a *Kiss concert*
As fat as a pig	- As fat as a *beer belly*
As black as coal	- As black as a *witch's cat*
As white as snow	- As white as *talcum powder*
As bright as a button	- As bright as *Shakespeare*
As cool as a cucumber	- As cool as a *marmalade cat*
As green as grass	- As green as a *witch's face*
As blue as the sea	- As blue as a *sapphire*

Now it's your turn, to turn that cliché into your very own super simile!

Naomi Craster-Chambers

Robin-Red And The Cat-Astrophe

Little robin redbreast singing sweet with pride,
Did not see the danger that was creeping by his side,
With one swift pounce the old black cat, put robin redbreast on his back.
The cat then smugly walked away, as on the floor poor robin lay.
The big black cat - the bullying thing!
Left Robin with a broken wing, poor Robin he began to shout,
'Please! Someone come and help me out.'

Pixie-bell was passing by and heard the little Robin's cry,
Pixie-bell the king of sound was helping robin on the ground.
On seeing Robin's broken wing, Pixie's bell began to ring,
Pixie knew his sound would mean the appearance of the fairy queen.
'Tell me, tell me,' said the queen, 'How Robin has done that?'
'Oh dearest, dearest fairy queen, it was old Astrophe the cat!'

The fairy queen was furious, her face turned red with rage,
'I'll have that Cat-Astrophe and teach him to behave.'
Soon she found old Astrophe purring deep with pride,
He did not see the fairy queen standing by his side.
With one swift swish her magic wand disturbed his happy sleep,
As he awoke and saw the queen! He curled up in a heap.

'You know that you've been bad,' she said, 'you know that you've done wrong.
How could you be so very cruel? What a way to carry on!
If I changed you into a bird, I think you would be sobbin',
What if I set a cat on *you* because *you* were a robin?'
At this old Astrophe did see, no way he wanted that!
So, there and then he promised her he'd be a better cat.

'Of course you will!' said the queen, she tapped his head and waved her wand,
She changed him from an old bad cat, into a kind and gentle one.
From that day on in Fairyland, all cats behaved the way they should,
There were no more Cat-Astrophes - they all were friendly, kind and good.

Marian Theodora Maddison

Cottage Friendship

The song shone brightly across the flagstone floor,
Through the glass panels of the red cottage door.
Molly rocked gently in the chair her Jim had made
Bess, her close companion and mate beside her laid.

Mary's thoughts were wandering back to the past,
When the working hours for her and Jim went fast;
The farm was their life, each animal their friend,
They looked after each other in their love to tend.

Each animal provided something towards its own keep,
Woollies were knitted from the coats of grazing sheep.
Eggs came from the chicken, and milk from the cows,
The pigs snorted loudly in the hay as they browsed.

Molly leant forward and fondled the ears of her Bess,
Of what her pet was dreaming, Molly could only guess;
Maybe controlling the sheep or a walk in the wood?
But now, without her master, she no longer could.

Then Molly slowly walked across the flagstone floor,
She momentarily paused, opening the red cottage door.
With Bess at her side, birds singing away in the trees . . .
She smiled, 'I'm so lucky to have such friends as these!'

Rosemary Boyd-Mercer

A Funny Little Squirrel

There's a funny little squirrel I know whose habits get jam on her head,
Her marmalade toes and blackberry nose comes from eating the bird-table bread.
Then one day she discovered a treat, all soft in the sunny day heat,
As she lapped up the honey she found it not funny, that her tail had stuck to her feet!

Joseph McGarraghy

The Princess And The Frog

A princess was out for her morning jog
When, by the pond, she met a frog.
She grabbed the poor thing by its head:
'It might turn into a prince!' she said.

She closed her eyes and made a wish,
Then gave the frog a sloppy kiss.
The princess counted one, two, three ...
And opened up her eyes to see.

In a blinding flash and clouds of smoke,
The frog became a handsome bloke.
He stared at the princess in dismay
Then turned and ran the other way.

'Wait, my darling, please!' she cried.
The handsome prince to her replied:
'Go stick your head in the palace bogs -
I hate a girl who kisses frogs!'

Melanie Ann Calvert

The Honeybee

When my mind is floating free,
I often hear a honeybee
Who sings thro' buzzy wings to me
A song in humming harmony
That tells of such a busy dizzy day!
Dashing wildly then to stall,
He listens to the flowers call;
Oh how their petalled heads enthral
In vibrant dance of bobbing wall
Inviting him to take their sweet buffet.

Mark R Slaughter

A Very Hungry Caterpillar

A very hungry caterpillar
Went crawling in the sun
His stomach started to grumble
So he ate an apple - one

Still hungry was the caterpillar
He wasn't sure what to do
So he went in search of juicy pears
And munched his way through two

On Wednesday he devoured plums
But his stomach was not merry
Found a patch of red delights
And ate four big strawberries

Five oranges down so juicy sweet
Was Friday's meal for him
But Saturday he ate some treats
That did not keep him thin

On Sunday his poor stomach ached
Full of all that food
He ate a leaf so big and green
That made him feel quite good

Now Caterpillar was not so small
And his appetite was now gone
He worked upon another task
And built himself a home

For two long weeks he stayed inside
Confined in his cocoon
At last he nibbled his way out
And emerged out of his room

What a surprise for this insect
As he flew into the sky
He'd changed inside his little home
And was now a butterfly!

With two wings full of colour
And antennae too like prongs
One very hungry caterpillar
Flew away, good luck, so long!

Helen Moll

Mischief Monster

There's a mischief monster in my school,
He wears dark shades and he acts real cool.
No one quite sees him. He's quicker than a fly;
Although, you might just catch a glimpse from the corner of your eye.

If you saw him you would see that he's dirty and he's grotty.
He does not brush his teeth and his nose is rather snotty.
He is dusty and he's musty and his name is Mouldy Mac,
And there's an awful patch of mushrooms growing on his back.

When the class is quiet, he can start to mess about;
Poking boys and girls to make them scream and shout.
Lunch break is his favourite time. He really is a sinner.
He loves to pick fleas off his chest and flick them in your dinner!

Mac plays tricks on teachers too. My teacher's called Miss Davy.
He takes her tea cup from her desk and fills it up with gravy.
He also stuffs the teacher's whistle up with cotton wool;
And then, when blown, to end playtime, no sound comes out at all.

Mac really is a monster, full of naughtiness and cheek.
Whenever he is bored it is mischief that he'll seek.
So the next time that you feel a little tap upon your back;
It may not be the person next to you, just bad old Mouldy Mac.

Wendy Farley

Prime Minister

If I became prime minister I think that I'd be good,
because I'd run the country the way I think I should.
I'd make it law for all grown ups to be in bed by eight,
but if we wanted to play with them, then bed would have to wait!
School would be but once a week and all we'd do is play -
and if I really wanted I'd make Christmas every day.
I'd give all kids a holiday with lots of ice cream too
and any grown ups who complained I'd put them in the zoo.
Chocolate, crisps or sweets for lunch, breakfast, dinner and tea,
if I became prime minister, I bet you'd vote for me!

Claire Holder

Ralphie And The Tree

Ralphie is a small boy who lives beside the sea.
He is a very friendly boy who is as happy as can be.

'It's nice to meet you everyone,' said Ralphie with such glee.
'Today's the day I first start school, so it's a special day for me.'

So Ralphie made his way to school with a smile on his face.
'Wow,' said Ralphie, 'so this is school, it's such a massive place.'

Ralphie waved his mum goodbye and then saw some books and toys.
So Ralphie went to see if he could find some other boys.

Then in the corner Ralphie found some boys who seemed quite glum.
'Come play with me,' Ralphie said, 'and we can have some fun.'

'Go away,' the boys all sneered, 'and don't make such a fuss,
we don't want you in our gang and you're too small to play with us.'

So Ralphie sat down in a chair, feeling hurt and sad.
'I know I'm small,' Ralphie said, 'but I'm really not that bad.'

But still the boys laughed in Ralphie's face, they called him short and dumb.
'I feel so alone,' Ralphie cried, 'I really want my mum.'

All day long Ralphie tried to join in with the boys.
'Go away,' the one boy said, 'you're too small to share our toys.'

Then the time came for Ralphie's mum to come and take him home.
'Oh Mum, why am I so small and dumb?' asked Ralphie with a groan.

Ralphie's mum looked shocked and said, 'Ralphie, you are just right,
you are not too small and dumb to me, you are the perfect height.'

Ralphie still felt sad and blue as he gazed out at the sea.
'I don't want to be small,' Ralphie said, 'I want to be tall like a tree.

The next day Ralphie walked to school wishing he wasn't so small.
'Stay away Ralphie,' another boy cried, 'you're too small to play with our ball.'

So Ralphie stood in the playground alone as sad as a boy could be,
when a voice said, 'Ralphie I'm your friend,' the voice came from a tree.

To Ralphie's surprise the tree could talk. The tree said, 'Ralphie, you listen to me,
I may be tall but years ago I was a smaller tree.'

The tree said, 'I once was a little seed and it took me time to grow,
but now I'm strong and I won't break if the wind should blow.

But when I was smaller and a seed that was sown, I wanted to be taller too,
I felt out of place and all alone, but it wasn't long before I grew.

You too will grow and become so strong, you may be the most splendid tree,
but you need to know it takes some time to become what you can be.'

'So I really will grow?' cried Ralphie with joy. 'I won't always be so small?
Oh thank you tree for telling me - you're the best friend of them all.'

So Ralphie kept his head up high and when the boys said, 'Ralphie you're too small.'
Ralphie said, 'You wait and see, I'll be taller than you all.'

To this the boys looked stunned and said, 'Well perhaps you can play with our ball,
perhaps you are the same as us, and all of us are small.'

So Ralphie made some friends that day and he's happy as can be,
but you must keep the secret safe of Ralphie and the tree.

Helen-Marie Saunders

A Crooked Take On An Old Tale
(Or 27 ways of being crooked)

There was a bent, dishonest man
who limped a convoluted mile
He found a purse of swindled gold
upon an old, distorted stile

And did he take it to the law
its rightful owner to be found?
Oh no, his thinking was askew
his moral outlook twisted round

He spent it on a cock-eyed cat
which caught a tiny, errant mouse
and they all lived obliquely in
a tumbling, wry, ramshackle house

And when the night was devious dark
they went a-stealing, sneaking down
the tortuous, bush-clad, zigzag hill
to vandalise and thieve the town

But when a curve of moon shone bright
they frolicked round the rotten house
that crooked man, the cross-eyed cat
the crazy, leery, little mouse

Carol Don Ercolano

Ballad Of Little Red Riding Hood

There was a girl with a blood-red cloak,
bluebells danced at her feet.
She thought that she would pick a bunch
for Grandma, as a treat.

She saw two eyes inside a bush,
dark as the ace of spades.
'Where are you going little girl?
No need to be afraid.'

'Off to my gran's.' He disappeared
to race the round half-mile;
his pounding heart as black as coal,
he leapt the crooked stile.

'Oh what big eyes you have, Grandma,
like full moons at midnight.'
'The better to see you with, my dear.
Come close and hug me tight.'

'Oh what big ears you have, Grandma,
and hairy as barbed-wire.'
'The better to hear you with my dear,'
smile like a damped-down fire.

'Oh what big teeth you have, Grandma,
like rocks on a stormy shore.'
'The better to eat you with, my dear.'
He rushed to bar the door.

The police broke in, arrested him.
'A woodsman phoned,' one said.
Red Riding Hood was driven home,
Gran bandaged, put to bed.

Peter Branson

Scavenger

A child is throwing a tantrum on the beach,
Annoyed by his lack of ice cream.
Meanwhile the tumbling sea retreats,
Leaving rock pools filled with dreams.

A toy gun that wouldn't work anymore,
Even if it had before;
A crab who's planning a cunning escape,
Although he'll be freed if he just waits;
A small toy dog all sandy and wet,
Now long overdue for its trip to the vet;
Dried up biros too wet to write,
A steaming match that had a fight
With the wide, blue ocean.

Rusty things that could be swords,
The bones of fish-like dinosaurs;
Something red that secretly lurks
Behind some used up fireworks;
Red, green, blue and old straw hats,
Collars of families' misplaced cats.
Maybe he finds them between the rocks,
Packs them up in a carrier box,
And sends the kittens home.

Who cares about ice cream
When this kingdom could be yours?
Not this little child
Who now plays out of doors.

Anastasia Symecko

Congratulations!

C aves of books stacked up high.
O ptical Express if your eyes hurt from the comp!
N ow and then, some sweets, one minute break.
G rinding through books.
R ampaging through time.
'A minute please!' You search through Facebook.
T ons and tons of Gold Information!
U p in that head, your infinite tube.
L umps on bellies, too much biology?
A nderson Shelters, what in the world?
T o say it through paper, through letter, through poem.
I t's hard to say, for a kid like me.
O n the day, the day of exams.
N ever tell me 'I've done bad!' Cos I know that you studied hard.
S o . . . stop stackin' those books! Take a break!

Delicia Ong

First Day

The time is drawing near,
my senses are tingling,
with a new-found sense of fear,
what will the next few days bring?
My mind has been ambushed,
by a million interlinking thoughts,
let's hope it turns out as I have wished,
in this new life I have sought.
The day has almost come,
perhaps I will come out of this not playing the fool,
maybe in fact it will be fun,
on the first day of my new school.

Kimberly Davidson

Noises In My Wardrobe

There's something in my wardrobe
I can hear it every night
Mum and Dad don't believe me
But it gives me quite a fright
Perhaps it is a monster
Something horrid with sharp teeth
I dare not look inside it
But I've often looked beneath
There's nothing underneath it
Nor on either of its sides
I think the top is empty
But inside it something hides
Perhaps it is quite harmless
I'd be safe to look and see
But on my own I'm frightened
Will you come and look with me?

Patricia Dixon MacArthur

Little Bo Peep 2008 Remix

Little Bo Peep has lost her sheep
She looked all over the UK
Then (being industrious) travelled the world
Until she reached the US of A.

She searched in all the fifty states
Came close in Texas, but found only cattle
Finally gave up and moved to the West Coast
Sheepless in Seattle.

Mark Niel

On Top Of The Hill

On top of the hill far away,
Duck, Donkey and Monkey went to play,
With a string on each tail they climbed up the hill,
Jimoma, Jimima that surely must kill!

Bubble and Squeak had too much to eat,
They needed some time to just chill,
So lay on your backs, it's time to relax,
Let the world go by on the hill.

Duck, Donkey and Monkey, Bubble and Squeak,
Didn't care about litter and that,
They trashed away without thought or delay,
Got bored and decided to go back.

As they walked down the hill with blistering feet,
Cursing the breakthrough of rain,
They fell on their rumps from the litter they dumped,
And cried from the guilt and the shame!

Fariah R Garner

Coniston Chickens

Inquisitive eyes stare at me,
Through the fence of wire.
They peck the ground, never tire
And do not long to be free.
The cockerel stands proud and tall
Protecting his hens with his call.
Majestic colours - red, green, fawn
Are passed onto any offspring born.
Their life seems so serene
Until one day, the fox has been.

Sandra Moran

Humour For Kids

There was a young girl with red eyes
All day she caught butterflies
In a net they'd go
To be put on show
They will never take to the skies.

There was a woman from Calcutter
She would only eat best British butter
She thought sunflower
Will have magic power
To get rid of her terrible stutter.

There was a ghost from Liverpool
Everybody thought he was a fool
He was so dim
They called him Tim
So he went back to fright school.

There was a boy with no brain
He would play out in the rain
The poor chap
He had a mishap
He slipped and fell down the drain.

Billy the kid was an outlaw
He was the best out of them all
He rode the west
A gun he used best
He was always the quickest on the draw.

Peter Pan didn't want to be a man
He went away as far as he can
He didn't need toys
He had the lost boys
Wendy joined and became their mam.

Michael McNulty

Mr And Mrs Grump

Mr Grump was a lazy brute who had holes in every single suit,
And Mrs Grump would curse and moan to her poor friends on the telephone,
'He's a useless fool!' she would declare. 'He won't even trim his nasal hair!'
Good for nothing, old Mr Grump. A hairy, spotty, human lump.
'What can you do, but eat and sleep?' Mrs Grump was often prone to weep.
'Burp and smell the whole day through. I wish I'd never married you.'
But Mr Grump had a gift unknown, yet his trumpet he had never blown,
For in his sleep, when deep enough, on comfy beds (or even rough),
He could snore aloud like no other, where Mrs Grump would run for cover,
Kick him, shouting, 'It's the sofa lad! No man could ever snore as bad
As you, foul beast, your savoury breath is worse than any grisly death!
The neighbours bang, they can hear you too! Please stop snoring or we're through!'
But Mr Grump was long and gone. His snores were like a rotten song,
Yet loud as bellows and foghorn wails, the air he breathed, as strong as gales.
The pickled eggs and cheesy crisps rippled through his snoring lisps.
So Mrs Grump could only beg, or desperately reach for her trusted peg
And clasp it firmly on her nose, a woman full of tired woes.
She placed a cork within each ear and gave old Grump a loving sneer.
'Sweet dreams you horror of a man. Of you I'm really not a fan.'
But Mr Grump could never hear. His dreams were full of fanatic cheer.
He'd scored again in the Snorer's Cup, and gone about ten-nil up!
Collected gold for the smelliest belch, coupled with a bottom squelch!
Mrs Grump at toss and turn, would never ever start to learn
That Mr Grump was more than zero. A sleeping, snoring, belching hero!

Steven Jackson

Chocolate Teddy Bears

I am one of several little teddy bears, standing in a row,
We are all made of sweet chocolate, covered from head to toe.
We all have the usual little features; eyes, ears, mouth and nose,
And around our necks we are wearing a red-ribboned bow-tie bow.

We have our own special box to travel in when we are bought from the display,
It could be a special present for someone . . . maybe for Easter, Christmas or even a birthday.
So, when you come into a chocolate shop, look for us standing in a row,
We are the little chocolate teddies, each of us wearing a red-ribboned bow-tie bow.

Mary Plumb

Billy Goat

This is the tale of a Billy goat,
Who was so frightened he jumped onto a boat,
He rowed and rowed until his arms were sore
And all because he was scared of a lion's roar.

He rowed all day way out to sea,
Until it was dark and he was hungry.
There was nothing to eat so he prayed to God,
And just as he finished, into his boat jumped a cod.

It's not the kind of thing he would normally eat as a rule,
But he was so hungry, he ate it until his belly was full,
He was so exhausted he slept as he bobbed up and down,
Although he was a bit cold as he didn't have time to bring a nightgown.

Day after day he rowed and ate fish,
But to be back on dry land was his wish,
Where will I go where it's not dangerous, thought Billy,
So he went as far as he could and ended up in Chile.

Neil Fowler

The Spider And The Fly

The spider and fly were best of friends
but this is where the story ends
One day the fly sat on the gate
along came the spider and the fly it ate

What went wrong, oh mercy me
couldn't the spider his friend he see
a juicy fly to tantalise
this was the spider's juicy prize

Some might say what a friend
the poor little fly came to an end
The spider now is a little fatter
daft as a brush, a little natter

Who would care, guess not you
the poor little fly was loyal and true
Watch your friend, be good and wise
don't end up in greedy eyes.

James Peace

Letter To China

On the way to school each day
I jump across a drain.
It always looks quite empty
apart, of course, from rain.

But I wonder where it leads to?
Does it run down to the sea?
If I dropped a letter in it
would it travel down - carefree

or would it join a lot of rubbish
and get mucky as it went
so that no one wants to read it,
such a soggy document!

But if I wrapped it up in plastic
it would stay quite nice and dry.
I would send it then to China
and the tides would make it fly

across the stormy oceans,
ending up upon the shore
of China - that's where you are Dad -
it could end up at your door!

It would tell you 'Happy birthday,
come home soon, if you can.
It's ages since I've seen you -
since before the term began'.

I'll send it off tomorrow,
well-wrapped so it won't leak.
I'll mark it 'Send to China' -
it should reach you by next week.

Rhona Aitken

The Helmet

I have a shiny helmet
it came in Santa's sack
'til now I have been sitting
in a seat on Mummy's back.

My mummy wants equality
no dolls or prams, I think
but Santa brought this helmet
in a bright and shocking pink!

I love my new pink helmet
it's the *best* I've ever seen
I even wore it up to town
when I went to see the Queen.

I wear it for our cycling
on Hayling Island's paths
and I *shan't* take my helmet off
even in the swimming baths.

I wear it for my dinner
to church, to shops, to bed
and I *shan't* take my helmet off
I'll keep it on my head.

I wore it to the doctors
I don't care what Mum said
I *shan't* take my helmet off
even when it's time for bed.

I put it on a week ago
and since that day I've grown
now Mummy cannot get it off
stuck fast it's ooh, ouch, groan.

Di Castle

Pick 'n' Mix Island

My chocolate log cabin, is my home
It is near a sherbet beach
With a lemonade sea
And a milkshake foam
It's the place I love to be
My garden is made of fondant cream
My path of peanut brittle
I have a coca-cola stream
And my one thousand and one weeds are little
The trees are made of chocolate logs
With leaves of boiled sweets
I even have a marshmallow dog
That I feed on doggy treats
With candyfloss clouds above
I sit here without a care
A marzipan bee and a coconut dove
Sit next to me, in my comfy liquorice chair
So why not come to my sweet shop isle?
All you have to do is dream
And I will take you on a lovely trip
And we will eat sweets, and lovely ice cream

Michael Shirt

There's A Goldfish In The Toilet

There's a goldfish in the toilet
We say a final prayer
Then Dad pulls the chain
And sends it to God knows where

Maybe it will swim to
Fish heaven, to joys we can't comprehend
Or maybe, like the last one
It'll get suck in the U bend

David Brady

The Tooth Fairy

I watch you sleep many a night
But this night you went all excited
I told you the story of the tooth fairy
And the thought of getting a treat pleased you

You had a wobbly milk tooth
That you wobbled all the time
And when it finally did fall out
You cried throughout the day

So I sat you down and told you a story
The tears stopped straight away
You ran upstairs to hide your tooth
Just like I had told you

I saw exactly where you placed it
So when you sleep I can swap it for a treat
You see my little one, I'm your personal tooth fairy
But you normally just call me mum.

Sharon Atkinson

The Boy Who Loved Sweets

There once was a boy who had big feet
and one day refused to eat veggies and meat.
'I only want food that is sweet,' he began to scream,
he decided to eat lollipops, chocolates and ice cream.
He soon became fat and terribly sick,
worried friends brought food and fruits very quick,
but he only wanted ice cream, chocolates and a lollipop on a stick.
He stopped eating sweets when his clothes could not fit
and he could not find a chair to sit.

Jerome Teelucksingh

Moonlit Memories

It's been an age since I have seen,
my friends the Bellifloe.
For men still hasten to destroy,
just like they warned me so.

Their trees were felled, their caves filled in,
then steamrolled firm and flat
to pave the way for yet more roads,
as if they wanted that.

And as for me, I'm all grown up,
my temples turning grey.
But deep inside the heart of me,
I long to sing and play.

I miss my jolly happy friends,
I miss their dayglo hair.
I miss their burping contest,
as their hats fly in the air.

I long for random silliness,
for jokes that make me cry.
I yearn to skip with daisy chains
and watching toadstools fly.

Alas it's true, their playfulness
we'll have to live without
for from this world they've upped and left,
of that I have no doubt.

But in a secret cubby hole,
all wrapped up safe and tight.
I've got a borrowed pogostick
and pray for one last flight.

Dickon Springate

The Girl Next Door

When I was a child
I gave her a chain
Of buttercups and daisies
I'd picked by the lane

The very next day
And to my surprise
She brought me a posy
The blue of her eyes

And told me the name
'Forget-me-not'
A long time ago
But I never forgot

The wind in her hair
The warmth of her smile
And a few fading flowers
I kept for a while.

J C Fearnley

Ladybird

Ladybird, ladybird
why so sad
munching leaves
you should be glad
Oh dear, oh dear
said ladybird
so glum
I've lost my spots
and I've lost my mum
Oh dear, oh dear
ladybird don't you see
you left them behind
when you went for tea . . .

Victoria Knowles

Isabelle The Dancer

This is about our great daughter called Isabelle
She might become a famous dancer, only time will tell
When you see that cheeky smile and that unforgettable grin
Her face will show her loveliness and charm will always win

Every time we see you princess, you give us a delightful pleasure
You are a charming child, one of this world's greatest treasures
That charming smile and your laughing eyes show your delight
You are that shining star that will appear in the dark of night

When you go on your adventure your wishes are never far away
You bring the happiness and laughter through those sunshine days
To your loving and devoted Mam and Dad you are that beautiful girl
You are precious and you are perfect like a sea washed pearl

Their comforting love and charming embraces are added to their list
When you go to your bed you will be rewarded with a goodnight kiss
Then have those wonderful dreams to be a dancer and singer
You can be a champion ballerina, to us you'll always be a winner

J F Grainger

Ketchup

You have me on bacon, fried eggs and spam,
I'm drizzled on sausages, warm bread and ham.
I'm smeared on chips and Friday's fried fish -
I'm the sauce that goes well with every dish!
I come in bottles and pots and jars,
I'm eaten in streets and cafes and bars!
I'm the most amazing sandwich filling,
When you say, 'Who wants ketchup?' then everyone's willing
to taste the red sauce - so delicious, so good!
I'm the world's greatest legend - I beat Robin Hood!
So - when you pop down and have ketchup for tea,
Just remember this poem and remember it's me!

Maria Dixon

Jessica's Cloud

'Look Mummy, look,
My name is written in the sky!
The letter J for Jessica,
You'll see it if you try.'

'Quick Mummy, quick,
Before the wind blows it away,
Let's take a photograph of it,
And send it off today.'

'We'll send it off to Grandma,
So that she can see it too,
A lovely fluffy letter,
In a sky of pretty blue.'

I got your photo, Jessie dear,
It makes me wish for you,
That all your days are sunny,
And that all your dreams come true.

Brenda Maple

Kinder Bear

When teddy bear
Falls out of his chair
I pick him up and say
There, there and into bed
With me he does come
'Neath covers deep
And we do sleep
With arms enfolded.

Robert Walker

Oral Hygiene

There was a naughty boy one day,
Who never cleaned his teeth.
Late one night they ran away
And haven't been seen since!

They ran to a land of no decay
Where they sparkled white and were brushed all day!

The boy was left with only gums,
He was the joke of all his chums.
He couldn't eat, he couldn't chew,
He just did not know what to do!

Then he awoke with a loud scream
And realised it was just a dream!

He rushed into the bathroom,
Not one second did he waste,
And grabbed his unused toothbrush
And covered it with paste!

He brushed every single tooth,
Until all squeaky clean,
Then smiled into the mirror,
The best teeth he'd ever seen!

Sonia Allen-Wall

The Birthday Party

Lots of bright balloons, all blown up by Dad
He did use a pump, he's such a jolly cad!
Furniture pushed aside, to make plenty of space
Streamers across the room - looks a different place!
Then a really long table with lots of little chairs
Plenty of room then for dancing children or bears!
So in comes yummy food, egg sarnies with jam
Sausage rolls and crisps, all made by my mam!
Crisps chips and pizzas, chocolate biscuits, fairy cakes
Tons of wobbly jelly, piled up upon paper plates
All the shouting and screaming, during exciting games
No falling out just yet until someone calls you names!
That certain song is sung as 'that cake' comes in
On top, seven little candles, lots of cheers make a din!
Cheeks puffed up with air, can the birthday boy succeed?
After all that lovely food, no help does he need!
Cake wrapped in serviettes, leave with each girl and boy
So tired after a birthday, even though so full of joy
Well, mountains of torn paper, window sills full of cards
Each one full of kisses from those family 'bards'
A sleepy head now rests, but not so for his mum
Gets the room back to normal, after all that noisy fun!
So when is it your turn? Happy, happy birthday to you
Always listen to your parents, they'll care all your life through

Maureen Westwood O'Hara

Door Key

On a walk with my new friend
We reached a path at the bend.
There was a gate in the wall,
Just like us, not very tall.
We entered by this little gate
And found an amazing garden state.
Wild bushes and grass so overgrown,
We were scared being there alone.
A rickety seat invited us to sit,
Where we found a small sandpit.
There was bucket, spade and tools
With a message to dig for lost jewels.
An old crone appeared at our side,
Telling us there was nowhere to hide.
We must discover a key of gold
To free ourselves of her real hold.
The door would unlock quite easily,
Once we had found the fitting key.
Someone was calling me from afar
And my own bedroom door was ajar.

Betty Bukall

Snowflakes

Snowflakes are delicate, soft and white,
Blowing around in the frosty night.
The way they fall
Means nothing at all.

They float around,
Not making a sound,
Tiny, gentle little flakes,
Landing on the garden rakes.

They are very hard to hold,
Even when they are wet and cold.
Snowflakes are now safe and sound,
They are safely lying on the ground.

Sherina Steele (10)

Unicorns

Unicorns exist it's true,
But you'll not find them at the zoo.
You won't find them in your local park,
They do not purr or even bark!
Unicorns exist it's true,
But you'll not find them at the zoo.
Unicorns love to gallop through the air
And to neigh at the moon so fair.
Unicorns exist it's true,
But you'll not find them at the zoo.
Unicorns adore silver and gold,
They're usually shy, occasionally bold.
Unicorns exist it's true,
But you'll not find them at the zoo.
They love the sparkle of tumbling streams,
Amongst waterfall rainbows they do dream.
Unicorn, unicorn, come to me,
Let's share joy eternally!

Amanda May Gazidis

Cat With Attitude

Long black whiskers, beady eyes and button nose
A cheeky look and a mischievous grin
In addition, little white patches and long fluffy fur
Jumping here, jumping there, all over the place without a care
Going through dustbins, cupboards and all
Settle down, here is a ball, but still you're my little cat
Tiny, little, muddy paw prints all over my clean floors
Miaowing and purring all the time
Go and play outdoors, is there no rest just for a while?
Even though you have attitude, you still make me smile.

David Alan Wheeldon

The Garage Sale

I went down to a garage sale
Some folks held down the road,
In hopes of finding bargains
To spruce up my abode.

The first stall had a bedside lamp
Without a bulb or plug,
And rolls of worn out carpet tiles
And tattered bits of rug.

The second had a one-wheeled bike
And rusted penny whistles,
A roller that had ceased to roll
And a brush without its bristles.

The third was selling dying flowers
And potted plants galore,
And what once was a tall proud fern
Was sadly not no more.

The fourth was full of sweets and cakes
Left out for way too long,
And far outdated fruit and veg
All going for a song.

The last was almost empty
Just a bowl full of water and lid,
And a sign said: *Invisible Goldfish!*
So I bought it for a quid.

Rick Bywater

Homecoming

muddied boots pause at the door
stamp moist dirt off the soles
then cross the threshold with brimming enthusiasm
stomp past the pine cabinet in the corner
past the umbrella stand
past two well-shined leather shoes
that hesitated for a moment before moving to the side
to let the boots pass
the boots continue on their journey
single-minded in direction
not slacking in their pursuit
of their destination:
the brown, plain-looking house shoes
situated next to chair legs
one final leap
the boots land next to the house shoes
complete a short frenzy of tap-dancing
then stop, and edge closer to the shoes
the house shoes turn
and next the boots rise up through the air
before slowing down and
swaying two feet above the shoes
as the little boy sits on his mother's lap
regaling her with his day's adventures

Hui Ying Ng

Lucy

It's Saturday morning, a dreary, wet day,
Caitlin and I want to stay in and play.
'I'm sorry,' says Mum. 'I'd like to stay too,
But there's no food in the house, we have shopping to do.
I know it's boring and I know it's a pain.
But it has to be done, so please don't complain.'
Why would we moan? We're not even peeved,
Because we have a weapon tucked up our sleeve.
A weapon so awesome there is simply no way,
We'll be going into town to do shopping today.

Her name is Lucy; she's really quite small,
It was only last week that she started to crawl.
Although she is little you would never believe,
The levels of destruction that she can achieve.

It takes a long time for us all to go out,
And involves lots of shouting and faffing about.
Finally we were ready; it's all gone quite well,
And then Mum notices the hideous smell.
'Don't look at me,' I say with a smile,
There's only one person who smells quite that vile.
'It can't be,' says Mum, her voice full of dread,
We all look at Lucy who is turning bright red.
Then the fun starts as she tries to crawl off,
And we chased her about with her nappy half off.

Finally we catch her and Mum cleans her up,
But then she starts screaming and will not shut up.
'Do you think she is hungry?' I say to my mum,
'If you look at the time, it's already past one.
That could be the reason she's in a bad mood,
Why not go to the shops once you've given her some food?'

Now Lucy and food, well what can I say?
My advice to you all is to keep well away.
If you want to stay clean and not get covered in muck,
It's best to stand back and be ready to duck.
By the end of her mealtime, Lucy's a mess,
There's food in her hair and all down her dress.
What is not on my sister is all over the floor,
The ceiling, my mother, the window and door.
Says Mum with a sigh, 'There isn't much doubt,
That we'll both need a bath before we go out.'

Lucy loves bath time; she thinks it is fun,
To splash about wildly and soak everyone.
The knack is to wash her quickly before,
The next tidal wave knocks you down on the floor.
She starts to scream loudly when we pull out the plug,
She won't let us dry her or give her a hug.
She wriggles so much that we can't get her dressed
Ten minutes later she's just wearing a vest.
'I wish she'd stop moving,' cries my mum in despair,
'Just long enough to get a comb through her hair.'
And if by magic Lucy sinks to the floor,
And in less than a minute she's started to snore.

Two hours later, she is still sound asleep,
By now my poor mother has started to weep.
'I don't understand it, it just isn't right,
That she sleeps in the day and keeps us up half the night.'
When Lucy wakes up, she is really not happy,
Mum checks her bottom; there's no poo in her nappy.
So we give her some milk and she drinks it so quick,
That once she had downed it, she's instantly sick.
'I give up,' says my mum. 'She's driving me beserk,
How can something so small, be quite so much work?
But surely this is the last change of the day
And nothing else will happen to cause more delay.'

Mum picks up Lucy, who is sat on the floor,
And holding her tightly makes a dash for the door.
'Hang on,' I say, 'I think something's wrong,
I might be mistaken, but can you smell a pong?'
Mum's face looks like thunder and she starts to shout,
'How can it be so hard for us all to get out?
But I won't be distracted, we have shopping to do
And we'll just have to take her smelling of poo.'
'But Mum,' I say, looking at my watch with a frown,
'Surely it's a bit late to go shopping in town.'
I smile at Caitlin and she smiles at me,
'We could go tomorrow,
But then again,
Let's see!'

Freya Morris

The Echidna

An echidna passed across a track
heading towards a special snack

A naturalist muttered, 'What a turn!
About this creature, I've got to learn.'

He kneeled to take a closer look
the echidna swung with strong right hook.

And it was such a heavy clout
It nearly knocked the watcher out.

The echidna curled into a prickly ball
snarling, 'I don't like you at all!'

The naturalist cried and mused upon
what it was that he'd done wrong.

He only wanted to see first hand
the weirdest creature in the land.

The echidna uncurled and stalked away
grumbling at his ruined day.

And idiots too dumb to know
you always let echidnas go -

About their business digging holes
and eating ants from salad bowls.

Or snufffling around a great big mound
where tasty termites are always found.

To spare echidna watcher's pain
the moral of this tale is plain.

Always remember it's very rude
to keep echidnas from their food.

Margaret Pearce

Letter To Santa

I bet your post bag's really full
Of letters from children like me,
Asking for presents and goodies
To be left by the Christmas tree.

I bet your postman's tired
Of carrying all your mail;
Do you leave mince pies for him
So that he will never fail?

Do you get lots of Christmas cards
And how about presents for you?
I think you should get the best
For all the hard work that you do.

So this year I will leave for you
A compass so you don't get lost
And an oil can for a smooth ride,
I'm not bothered about the cost!

There'll be an umbrella for the rain
And a street map of my home town,
I'll mark my street and house so you
Don't end up driving around.

Finally, dear Santa I'll leave you
A flask of tea and toast to eat
So that on Boxing Day you can
Relax and enjoy my little treat.

Sue Gerrard

Daisy And The Goat Coat

Daisy the cat had spent her life living in total fear of the rain and she decided that she had had enough. After a quick catnap, she decided to visit her good friend Emma the mountain goat. So off she ran, passing through the forest of no trees, which was actually a field! She finally arrived at Emma's straw house. She scratched at the door (as it was pointless to knock). Emma answered almost immediately and lead Daisy inside. Well, Daisy didn't waste any time and came right out with it, about the fact that she was terrified of the silver droplets that came from the floating marshmallows in the sky. It took Emma a moment to figure out that Daisy was talking about rain! So she sat Daisy down and explained that everyone gets the collywobbles about something and that her own fear was that of spiders. As a treat, and to cheer Daisy up, she gave her some catmint flavoured goats' cheese and a waterproof woolly raincoat made from the finest goats' hair available (in other words, her own!) so that the next time it rained, Daisy should eat some of the cheese, which would help her feel relaxed and dream, and then put on the waterproof goat-coat, which would help keep Daisy dry, and as a favour, could Daisy chase out all the spiders? Daisy happily agreed and next time it rained, Daisy didn't feel quite as scared as she used to.

Jeremy Bloomfield

An Introduction To Charlie Cheshire

Charlie Cheshire is a very wise man and works for the local newspaper 'The Wensleydale Gazette'. He knows what is happening most of the time, and nearly everyone in the Vale he has met.

His job is to discover what's going on in the place and to write interesting and useful local news, and he loves his job, investigating and reporting, and finding out about other people's views.

He's good at his job, fantastic with people, and is married with a beautiful young daughter. He worked very hard to get to where he is, and is very proud of his job as a reporter.

He went to a local school, called Gorgonzola High and was taught to be honest and true, and if Charlie says he'll do something, then that's exactly what he'll go and do.

Derek L Owen

The Witch And The Mouse

I looked up at the sky tonight
and the moon was shining silvery bright
the stars were twinkling in the sky
and then . . . I saw a witch fly by!
She gave a cackle and then a scream
as she flew across the moon's bright beam,
so I stood very still in the bright moonlight.
I didn't want the witch to catch me tonight.
I waited as quietly as I could
I wanted to make sure she was gone for good,
and when I tiptoed across the moonlit green
I suddenly heard her wicked scream!
She swooped upon me from the skies
and had a strange look in her eyes.
I ran off as fast as I could
heading for the safety of a distant wood.
I ran really fast, I tried to flee
but wherever I went, so did she!
'Stop! Stop!' I heard her call
but I wasn't going to stop at all!
I kept on running as fast as I could
and headed for the safety of the wood.
I'd hidden behind a great big tree
hoping the witch wouldn't see me
but I was wrong, and she found me that night,
and all I could do was shake with fright!
She took hold of me by my shirt
and promised that I wouldn't be hurt.
'I'm not a wicked witch, you see,
and I'd like you to do a little job for me.'
Her magic broomstick was by her side.
'Get on,' she said, 'we'll go for a ride,
hold on though, it's a long, long flight,
but don't worry, you'll be home tonight.'
We travelled higher and higher into the sky
even higher than the birds could fly,
far beyond the moon, so bright
ever deeper into the night.
From the Milky Way to Saturn's rings
I saw so many wonderful things.
Stars of gold and silver and white,
and stars that lit up the whole dark night.

On and on sped the witch's broom
until finally we came to a large red moon.
'This is the place I want you to see,'
Said the witch, over her shoulder to me.
We landed by a river that was green,
quite the strangest thing I'd ever seen.
The trees were blue, with leaves that were white
and the grass was as dark, as the darkest night.
She took me to a very strange place,
a house that was made of green ginger and lace.
Chocolate bars made the door,
and there were candyfloss carpets on the floor.
The witch took a box from a drawer
and pointed to a hole in the floor.
'There's only one thing wrong with my house,
down in that hole, there lives, a mouse!
I want you to capture that mouse for me
and then put it in this box you see.
I'd do it myself but they scare me so
and without your help, it will never go!'
I said, 'You're a strange witch, to be frightened of mice,
I've got two at home and I think they're nice.
I'm sure if you try, you'll overcome your fear
and learn to like the mouse that lives here.'
The witch asked, 'Do you think I could really do that?
I haven't had a pet, since I lost my cat.
It would be nice to have a pet in the house,
okay then, I'll try not to be afraid of the mouse.'
I captured that little mouse with ease
because it couldn't resist a large slice of cheese.
It was the strangest mouse I'd ever seen
with fur that was coloured red and green!
The strange little mouse ate all the cheese
and then he squeaked, 'More please!'
'Oh how wonderful!' I said. 'A mouse that can speak.
It's going to be so much easier for you two to meet.'
The mouse looked at me and his nose gave a twitch,
'Do you mean,' he said, 'that I've got to meet the witch?'
'Yes,' I said, 'but she's afraid of mice
and you've got to show her, that you're very, very nice.'
The strange little mouse said, 'It would be nice,
if the witch could learn to like little mice.'
And then he said, as his nose gave a twitch,
'I think I'd like to be friends with the witch.'

'You're very welcome to stay in my house,'
Said the witch to the strange little mouse.
'I'm sure if I try hard my fears will disappear,
and life for us then should be very happy here.'
The mouse and the witch danced with glee,
and then she announced it was time for tea.
We sat down to a table set to please
and just for the mouse, there was special green cheese!
After plenty of games and lots of fun
the witch announced my job was done.
She said, 'It's time for you to leave, my friend,
your little adventure has come to an end.
I'd like to thank you for coming to my house
and helping me make friends with the mouse.
Without your help I'd still be alone
and I wouldn't have the mouse, as a friend, in my home.'
The witch waved her wand above her head
and I couldn't understand the words she said.
There was a flash and a bang, and I was standing alone,
outside the front door, of my very own home!
Now, I've told you a story that's really grand
of my adventure in the witch's land,
but who would believe what I've been through?
Now, tell me the truth . . . really . . . would you?

Stephen Sell

Christmas Poem - Guess Who?

A jolly fellow
Dressed in red
He visits you
Whilst you're in bed
Once a year
He drives his sleigh
To bring you toys
On Christmas Day.

Sue Hardiman

One Lemon Lolly

One lemon lolly, melting in the sun,
Two fat flies on a stale currant bun.
Three blue buttons, doing up your coat,
Four saucy sailors, singing on a boat.
Five pairs of pants, blowing on the line,
Six cuckoo clocks, telling you the time.
Seven great gorillas, playing in the zoo,
Eight brass bells, shiny, bright and new.
Nine cheeky chickens and one red hen,
Add them all together and that makes ten!

Catherine Robinson

The Giraffe's Unfortunate Fear

In the plains of the Lake Albert delta,
Lives a giraffe plagued by the most terrible fear,
He's calm and controlled when not standing,
But terror is always quite near.

All the other giraffes do tease him,
Because what brings on this case of frights,
Is that the poor chap suffers from vertigo,
The only giraffe scared of heights.

Rob Waugh

Tripity Pat

Tripity Pat fell down flat,
head over heels on a snoozy cat.
The cat took fright,
ran right out of sight
and didn't come back 'til the following night.
'Poor Puss,' said Pat, 'he must think I'm rotten.'
But Puss still loves Pat, so he must have forgotten.

Marvis Lyn-Dahl

Monsters

Late at night when you rest your weary head
No goblins will come to tickle your toes
No witches will come to tweak your nose
As there are no monsters under the bed

Late at night when you rest your weary head
No ghouls will come to give you a fright
No gremlins will keep you awake through the night
As there are no monsters under the bed

Late at night when you rest your weary head
No phantoms will dare come to keep you awake
No werewolves will come to see what they can take
As there are no monsters under the bed

Late at night when you rest your weary head
Angels and fairies will help you to sleep
Through golden slumbers with dreams that are yours to keep
As there are no monsters under the bed

Late at night when you rest your weary head
Say goodbye to your troubles and wish your worries away
Tomorrow will be a brand new glorious day
And remember there are no monsters under the bed!

Nia Glyn Williams

Old Man Fred

There is a man called Old Man Fred,
Who wears an apple on his head,
Banana shoes, pineapple tops,
Strawberry coat and green grape socks,
Orange pips on his coat zips, lemon zest on his string vest,
A tangerine to keep him clean, I've rarely seen a stranger scene,
But Old Man Fred he aims to please,
With a pair of pears strapped to his knees,
A rhubarb stick around his waist,
A slice of lime stuck on his face,
And last of all but don't tell Mum,
A big fat plum stuck to his bum!

Scott Holroyd

Ruth The Tooth Fairy

There's a fairy called Ruth,
That collects every child's tooth,
To help build her castle,
She swaps the tooth for a parcel,
A special fairy gift,
On every night time shift,
Ruth visits every child,
Boy or girl,
Fantastic or wild!
A child in India or Rome,
Each child in bed asleep in their home,
And once she has swapped their tooth for a parcel,
She flies all the way home again to her tooth castle,
She adds the new tooth to a wall or a beam,
And snuggles down in her bed for a magical dream.

Alicia Longcroft

Friends

Friends are forever in sickness and in health
Friends support each other through thick and thin
Friends laugh together through the sunshine and the rain
Friends will grow closer through the heartaches and the pain.

Our friendship knows no boundaries, our friendship has no ends
As friends we'll always find a way to make amends
I'll be your friend in hardship and desperate times of woe
I'll be there to defend you as we onward go.

When you are feeling lonely, down trodden and despair
Remember all the good times we had because we care
Today we'll sit together and reminisce about the past
As we go on together our friendship will last and last.

Margaret Archer

The Weaver

'Who taught you how to spin dear?'
'Who taught you how to spin?'
'Mothers wove it in me - deep threads embedded

Here in the weaving space of dreams
She flows like water in the rocks;
The weaver

How old? How young? To weave such dreams
Spinning the threads of sunlight through the splashing sea
And dragging it forward; to make a cloth upon a rocky place.

And what a cloth of seaweed strands and limpet jewels
To sit upon and dream
'Of what do you dream?'

'Of other places far away and warm'
'Of mothers fussing'
Then the wind drifts by and that dream goes -

The weaver's eyes upon a bird,
fly free across the rocky place,
She is carried to the palace high above this cold place -

Home to the woven palace - far away and warm
To mothers fussing
Who teach her how to spin.

Kal (Karen Alicia Louise Burt)

Number 9

I thought he was
A friend of mine
That silly, squiggly
Number 9

But, I've watched him
He's up to tricks
Sometimes he is the
Number 6.

Heather Sneddon

Teddy Land

Take my hand and walk with me
When sleep has closed your eyes.
I'll take you to a land of dreams
Where the Teddy bear walks and flies.

We'll paddle our feet in crystal streams
As Teddy fish float by,
While Teddy birds will take to wing
On thermals, rising high.

I'll show you herds of Teddy bears
Like drifting clouds on land,
Then I will let you pick one out
To stroke and feed by hand.

Then we will have a picnic,
Where the guests are Teddy bears,
With fun and food and party games,
Like tag and musical chairs.

Take my hand and walk with me
When sleep is playing its game,
I know the place where Teddy bears
All wait to know your name.

Pete Sparrow

Baboon

On a wonderful spring afternoon
I encountered a charming baboon.
We rambled for miles
sharing fruit cake and smiles -
we get married one Sunday next June!

Matt Goodfellow

Wear The Sunshine In Your Heart

From time to time you may feel sad
When in your life some things are bad
Take this sample for example
Rainy days and upset tums
Guarantee to make you glum
So if you're down and feeling blue
What is best for you to do

Wear the sunshine in your heart
And banish sadness from the start
Laughter is the best of tonics
Giggles of course are only platonic
When you proudly wear a grin
Unpleasant things don't seem as grim
A chuckle helps to make you feel good
Quite fit and proper to know that it should

It's wise to be jolly and full of glee
These are emotions you want to keep
And when you smile you're on a roll
You'll feel contentment in your soul
Leave behind your trouble and strife
Enjoy instead your great gift of life
Always remember what ever you do
There's always one less fortunate than you

Gary Raynes

The House Of The Woodland Creatures

Little wolf who rides the night
In which direction do you run?
To north, to east?
Or south or west?
Or do you chase the clouds by day
And by night the stream?
And if the moon is full and round
Do you really howl and scream?

Little Elf who plays by day
And makes mischief in the woods,
Are you good,
Or bad, or both?
Or are you quite the opposite,
The woodland's pride and joy?
The cherub of the Earth and sky
And nature's little boy?

And little house built brick by brick,
Are your chimneys quite secure?
Are you warm
And soft, and bright?
Or are you none of the above
And cold, and sad, and dead?
But no, I know that you'll be there
When all is done and said.

Vida Adamczewski

Twinkletoes

In the enchanted wood, mother cat took her kittens to a new safe home, accidentally leaving one behind. Fairies found her, named her Twinkletoes, and gave her magical powers to protect them from the witches' cats that caught fairies in the wood. The witches shook the magic dust from the fairies so they couldn't fly anymore.

One day Twinkletoes followed a cat to an old cottage and was caught by two other cats. She struggled as she got pushed through the big wooden door, and three warty faces with large hooked noses stared down at her with orange eyes. They cackled as they pushed her into a cage. She saw four of her fairy friends tied up in the corner as the three witches started to chant. Twinkletoes clawed her way through the cage bars and freed her friends. They pointed to a bright light coming from a table. 'That jar contains our fairy magic that the witches have taken from us.' As Twinkletoes slunk across the room towards it, one of the witches saw her and tried to catch her, but Twinkletoes flew into the air, round and round and made the witch giddy. Twinkletoes grabbed the jar, threw it on the floor, smashing it into a hundred pieces. Magic swept over everything, the witches turned into princesses and the cats recognised Twinkletoes as their sister.

The fairies had their magic back and flew home. The princesses ran back to their castle where they were greeted with great joy.

Linda Knight

James' First Christmas

Snowflakes fell from the midnight sky as Santa arrived with his reindeer.

'Oh for the days when houses had *real* chimneys,' Santa grumbled.

Nowadays Santa had to enter through windows. So with sack over shoulder, Santa entered the darkened house. Only baby James stirred to greet Santa.

'These musical teddies are much sought after,' Santa told James. 'Your parents ordered one weeks ago for you.'

James gave Santa one of his golden smiles; he looked just like a cherub.

'All babies are cherubs,' Santa told his apprentice elf. 'James' parents thought they would never have a baby.'

Cherubs are everywhere from Christmas cards to paintings. Babies are cherubs given straight from God to parents as a Christmas gift all year round.

Catherine Keohane

Rabbit And Me

I spied a little meadow
With a little shady tree
It had a little stream
So peaceful and luv-er-ly.

Sheep were grazing
The birds were singing
And frisky little lambs
Were playing or snoozing.

I sat on the grass
Under the little tree
And a little baby bunny
Came hopping up to me.

'Hello,' said Bunny
'Hello,' said me
'Would you like to join me
And share my tea.'

I unpacked my picnic basket
And gave him a carrot
And we sat by the stream
Chatting for hours.

It started to get dark
And he looked at his watch
'I better be going
Before I'm eaten by a fox.'

We said our goodbyes
And off the bunny hopped
Now I'm going home
To wash my smelly socks.

Anne D Morgan

Football

Football glides through the air
Travelling with grace and passion
Like an eagle on its travels
Then the silence of this moment
Is shattered by the thundering
Of boys' heavy boots piercing
Immaculate green mown lawn.

He measures his strides meticulously
And the ball falls at his feet
He twists and turns around his man
And eases himself forwards
Like a lion he spots his target
And pulls his right leg back
With a powerful strike
Leather meets leather
And again the ball takes flight.

Expectant faces watch its journey
And a roar explodes all around
White net ripples catching its prey
A goal to clinch the victory
Striker turns on his heel
Fist held up in glory
Face contorted roaring in ecstasy

Rapturous team mates spring to
Engulf him sharing in his emotion
This glorious English game of boys and men
A spectacle capturing our senses and
Enrapturing our emotions on a
Warm, spring Sunday morning.

Lizzi Simpson

Camping

We've come out camping - silly us
We wish we hadn't now, because
The sun's gone in, the rain's come down
So heavily we nigh on drown.
We struggle to take out our tent
And see the fifty pounds we spent
Were wasted, as the tent has soaked
Up all the water. With a croak
We start the fight to build the thing
But with a rather fierce fling
The sides collapse, the pegs come loose
'Pick them up, you silly moose!'
'It's your fault; don't try blaming me!'
'Your side's falling, can't you see?
'Just hold it straight - not wonky - straight!'
'Hurry up, it's getting late!'
'I'd be long done if you weren't here!'
'If you'd not taken half a year . . . '
'You're getting water over me!'
'Nonsense, it dripped off the tree.'
'I hate this tent. How much was it?'
'It doesn't matter. Grab this bit.'
'We're never going to get this built . . . '
At last we do, though there's a tilt
To the top, and to the side
And even, somehow, the inside.
There's not much space; it's wet and cold,
Tempers fray, we curse and scold.
Drift off into uneasy sleep
As rainwater beings to seep
Into the tent, which makes things worse
The atmosphere stays tight and tense.
When morning comes and the sun rises
The unfortunate surprise is
The tent has gone, blown far away
And - soaking - in the field we lay.
Miserable and frozen limbed
Camping fantasies have dimmed
Into nothingness. We go
Back home, our footsteps short and slow
And we both make a silent vow
That from today - beginning now

We'll never come again to camp
On a day so cold and damp
As this one, and next time we went
We'd get ourselves a decent tent.

Eleanor Hough

The Boxing Match

The Collie and the Boxer dog were spoiling for a fight -
The Collie told his punchy pal, 'I'll box your ears, alright?'
The Boxer, somewhat taken aback, stood up to his full height,
Then strode towards the Collie and lashed out with all his might.

The Collie's eyes were fast and sharp - he swiftly stepped aside,
The Boxer, neatly caught off-guard, fell down and bruised his pride,
This got the fighter's temper up - he almost heaved up lunch
Then thrashed the air with rapid paws - but couldn't land a punch.

On seeing this, the Collie laughed and showed his Sheepdog Shuffle
Then kept the Boxer well at bay (whilst sucking on a truffle),
As minutes passed, the Boxer tired - he felt like such a fool,
So Lassie showed him sympathy with first aid - cotton wool.

And then, in time, they sat aside to talk their problems out,
The Collie waited patiently and let the Boxer pout.
'I can't believe,' the Boxer cried, 'I couldn't land a paw!
With all my fighting expertise, I'm feeling rather sore.'

The Collie then explained to him a simple sheepdog rule,
'When bringing in the herd at night, one has to maintain cool . . . '
'That's fine when picking up a girl - not fighting, I'm afraid,'
The Boxer gave a churlish look - and then removed his shades.

Nick Masters

Scary Monster

What's behind that grate in the wall?
Is it a monster big or small?
Past my feet the cold water flows
Did I just see green eyes glow?
Can I hear breathing short and sharp?
Can I see a shape back there in the dark?

I should leave, but something makes me stay
Please don't grab me, I silently pray
I shiver as sweat rolls down my back
I pull a torch out of my rucksack
I turn on the light, afraid of what I might see
I jump at the big scary rabbit looking back at me

I laugh at myself and jump to my feet
I whistle all the way home and smile with relief
My scary monster turned out to be fluffy and cute
And not a seven foot tall, scary brute
Fear and darkness played tricks with my mind
Turn on the light, there's nothing scary to find.

Alan Brafield

A Treasure Hunt

I want to find buried treasure
That a pirate left long ago
I wonder where to look for it?
I wonder if you know?
I've dug up the garden, there was no treasure there
I've looked in the cupboard under the stairs
I've ransacked the attic and that was bare
Apart from cobwebs and a broken chair
So where would a pirate leave his loot?
I've checked in the garage and the car boot
I've searched the toy box and the fridge too
I've even looked in the downstairs loo
But I can't find treasure anywhere
So I'll hide some myself, and if you dare
You can look for the treasure, and if you guess
You can help me tidy this awful mess!

Luna Deller

My Friend Dragon

My best friend is a dragon
He doesn't shoot fire or roar
Although he's really quite interesting
He's also a bit of a bore

He knows about maths and history
He tells the time by the sun and moon
How he knows these things is a mystery
I wish he'd teach me . . . and soon

Then I wouldn't have to go to school
And learn things like English and French
I wouldn't be told off by teacher
And sent to sit on the 'quiet bench'

I wish I was clever like Dragon
Then I wouldn't be in this fix
He's my very best friend, is Dragon
Even though I'm only six

Suzan Round

Happily Ever After

They lived happily ever after,
Hidden in their castle.
All the villagers were baffled,
One after another they would gather.

Despite him being handsome, but poor,
They lived happily ever after,
Nothing was dafter,
Than the jaws that dropped to the floor.

She had golden hair, so long and thick,
That nothing that could grow faster,
They lived happily ever after,
In their house of marble and brick.

Their home was filled with laughter,
Due to his kindness and her sense,
Their love was a kind so dense,
They lived happily ever after.

Kasongo Swana (15)

The Last Toy

Thingy was a lonely toy. He did not look like the other toys, or any toy for that matter. He lived in the Old Toyshop, never been bought and unloved.

'I wish someone would buy and love me,' Thingy said to the other toys, but they just laughed.

'No one will want you,' they remarked.

Christmas was approaching and the other toys were disappearing from the shelves, to be cherished. After closing time, Thingy sat alone on an empty shelf. Looking outside the shop window, he could see shoppers passing, not interested in him. A young girl with ragged and worn clothes approached the window. She shivered at the cold. Thingy looked longingly at her, the young girl looked back, smiling.

As the days passed, Thingy was always the one left on the shelf. Each night he looked sadly out of the window, each night the young girl would appear at the window, smiling. Thingy felt joy for the first time.

On Christmas Eve, as more toys were bought, Thingy remained on the shelf. As the Old Toyshop was ready to close, the young girl stepped in, trembling from the cold outside. 'How much is that toy?' she asked the shopkeeper, pointing towards Thingy.

'How much do you have?' asked the shopkeeper, smiling.

Opening her hand, she revealed a small number of coins. Taking just one, the shopkeeper smiled and handed Thingy to her. The girl grabbed Thingy and hurried out of the Old Toyshop, cuddling him.

Thingy smiled joyfully.

Martyn Harrison

Susie And The Dinosaur

Once upon a time there lived a little girl named Susie. Susie was an ordinary little girl who liked to play with her dollies and read her story books.

One day Susie was sat outside in the garden playing with her favourite dolly, Bethany, when she heard a rustling in the bushes. Susie looked around but she couldn't see anything so Susie went back to plaiting her dolly's hair. Again she heard the rustling. Susie stood up and looked about but saw nothing. Susie put her hands on her hips and kept looking about.

The bushes rustled again and this time Susie saw something. She watched the bush as she saw it move again seeing a green tail, Susie wasn't afraid though. She walked up to the bush when all of a sudden something jumped out of it. Susie jumped back, surprised. She looked down at the floor to see a baby dinosaur. It was green and very little. The dinosaur looked back up at Susie. Susie bent down and held her hand out to the dinosaur. The dinosaur smiled and Susie stroked it. Susie smiled and said, 'I think I'm going to call you Bob.' The dinosaur smiled at her as she picked Bob up and stroked him. Susie went into the house and showed her mummy the dinosaur.

Susie's mum smiled at Susie and Bob and said, 'Hello Bob, would you like to stay for tea?'
Susie and her mum laughed as Bob smiled.

Katrina Miles (14)

My Medical Appointment

I was out at the doctor's, a medical appointment,
Missed double science, a real disappointment,
Oh happy days, school is away,
I'll scream out in joy, 'Hip, hip, hooray!'

The doctor said, 'You've got the flu.
You'll need to stay off school, today, tomorrow too.'
When I thought tomorrow was a time to relax,
I remembered the match and stopped in my tracks.

'I don't mind today, but tomorrow is bad.
I'll be well tomorrow, I'm a healthy lad.'
'I think you'll be worse, you should stay inside,'
He took my hand then deeply sighed.

'But I've got to be there, I'm the team head,
I'll be really good, and go early to bed!
I'll go to church, and ring the bell,
I'll tidy my room and Hoover as well.'

'I'm sorry my boy, but it has to be,
I'd try to help, I would really!'
It seems that now, I don't feel so cool,
I wouldn't miss the match if I'd stayed at school.

Chloe Cox (13)

Isobel's Song

My mummy will feed me and bathe me each day.
She'll love me and soothe me, tuck in my duvet.
My daddy will shield me, keep evil at bay.
He'll love me and protect me and show me the way.

My grandmas will love me and be there when I stay.
They'll nurture me, 'You'll be alright,' they'll say.
My grandpas will love me and watch me at play.
They'll teach and advise me in case I should stray.

I will need all of these as I go through my life.
I will call on them all to keep me free from strife.
I'll think of them and as I reach my due time.
I'll thank them and love them and enter my prime.

My mummy, my daddy, my grandparents too,
will teach me and help me learn what I must do,
to be strong and be wise, and as I try to get through,
they'll teach me as well to be caring and true.

Yes, I'll need all of these as I travel my road.
What they will have given me will lighten my load.
I will love them and then when and if its my due,
I'll remember them all when *my* baby is due.

David Wall

Bragavere Saves The Day

Bragavere lay on the lush grass drumming his claws on a nearby stone. He snorted, dislodging a pesky butterfly who had landed on his snout, again. Being young and agile made Bragavere perfect for the job of Border Patrol - where magic meets reality. But lazing around did not suit him, he wished for action and adventure - patrol was very unexciting.

His excellent hearing alerted him to distant crying. Immediately he rose, stretched and flexed his wings, drew in a deep breath and took flight. Bursting through the cloud barrier, Bragavere could see a young girl stranded on a ledge. A snapping cracking sound told the young dragon the ledge would soon give way. 'No time to lose,' he told himself, diving deeply and swiftly to the rescue.

Amy tried to remain brave but as the sun started to set her courage began to falter. Surely her gran was missing her. The noise of flapping wings caught Amy's attention. Slowly she turned her head and came face to face with … a dragon!

Razor-sharp teeth glinted. Amy was snatched off the ledge. She fainted, much to the relief of Bragavere. 'Good, can't do with all the flailing and screaming. Anyway, I'm not hideous!'

Circling down to a field near the village he deposited Amy carefully on the grass. Then up and away into the darkening sky.

Opening her eyes, Amy stared desperately trying to figure out the silhouetted shape in the sky. It couldn't be a dragon, just couldn't, could it?

Paula Cassidy

Connor And His Tractor, Ted

Calling for his faithful sheepdog, Sandy, Connor hurried into the yard. Ted, the tractor, had enjoyed the break because they had been leading straw and hay all morning, ready for bedding and feed for the animals during the cold and snowy winter months. In fact, Ted knew that, without him, Connor could not manage to do all the work there was on the farm, which made him feel very proud and important.

'Hi Ted, here we go again,' said Connor, as he, followed by Sandy, jumped into the driving cab. Switching on the engine, Connor drove off towards the fields to check on the animals, walls and fences, as they did every day. 'Well Ted,' said Connor, 'I wonder what we'll find today?' Ted loved it when Connor spoke to him like a friend, and he gave a little cough as they rolled along.

Suddenly, Sandy barked, as she ran towards a sheep with a broken hind leg. Connor gently picked it up and placed it carefully on Ted's trailer, before driving slowly back across the field, with Sandy sitting on guard. On his mobile phone, Connor called for a vet to treat the animal, which they did within an hour.

After another long day, Ted felt his engine swell with pride as Connor patted it saying, 'Well done, I couldn't do without you. We'll have another adventure tomorrow. Night-night!'

Anne Maureen Simpson

Legend

Epheus Martin sat on the wall
Staring at space, contemplating it all
When, from the woods in the distance, he heard such a wail
He turned 'round in dread to see who was in ail

Out through the trees ran a young forest child
Her hair vibrant and red, her clothes ripped and wild
'You sir, you sir!' yelled she to the man
Tears streaming like rain from eyes of cyan

Epheus asked, 'What troubles you, my dear?'
'There's a beast that makes the children disappear,'
She told him, with fear lacing her voice
And when he saw her sweet eyes, he had no choice

'That shall happen no more,' Epheus declared
And with his sword and his bow, he was more than prepared
'But tell me young one, what is thy name?'
'Ember,' said she, 'for my hair is like flame.'

To the forest centre, our hero departed
And the sight of the beast 'twas not for faint-hearted
Fur covered every inch of its humungous being
And if you saw its teeth you would be fleeing

It was the colour of dead trees, its eyes like the moon, trapped
With fangs like axes, and claws like twigs, snapped
It roared like the wind that fells trees, when it saw the pair
'I am the death of the forest, I am the tree rot, the axe man, the despair

I take the souls of the forest children, just like the hunter takes a deer with his bow
And I've wanted that girl with hair like a raging fire, since a long time ago.'
But Epheus aimed and shot an arrow straight in the moon of the great beast's eye
His sword slashed the beast and it fell with a piteous cry

Young Ember danced with her forest chums, writing songs of joy on their guitars
And Epheus walked on, content with his word, and no longer gazed at the stars

Zoë Richardson

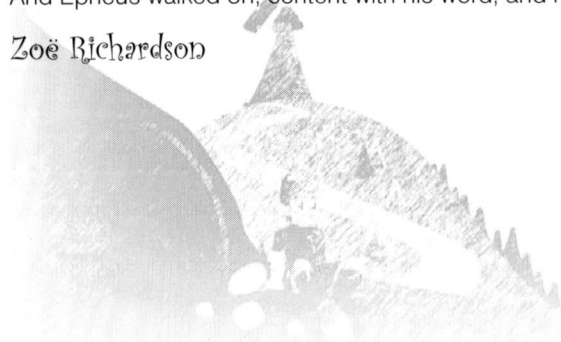

Jasper The Cat

This is the story of Jasper the cat
Who was lazy and sleepy and terribly fat.
He would sleep in the cupboard or under the chair
Or out in the garden - he hadn't a care.

But one day, at teatime, he couldn't be found
So Sally, his owner, she searched all around
She looked in the cupboard and under the chair
She looked in the garden, but he wasn't there.

She searched in the bathroom and under the beds
She asked the neighbours, but they shook their heads
'We haven't seen Jasper around for a while.'
Poor Sally was sad, but she gave them a smile.

'He has to be somewhere, I'm sure he'll appear,'
And she carried on walking while wiping a tear.
She walked up the road to the old village green
But Jasper was not anywhere to be seen.

'Oh Jasper,' she sighed, 'you have caused such a fuss.
I'm so worried about you, my wandering puss.'
She climbed up the hill to the edge of the wood
Where the bluebells were growing and the tall trees stood.

She called out his name but it echoed right back
Then looked for his paw prints in the muddy old track
She saw rabbits and owls and a brown oily rat
But there was no sign of Jasper, her lovely black cat.

She searched in the playground and then in the park
But had to go home before it got dark.

As she sleepily climbed into bed that same night
She pulled back the covers and turned out the light
And there on the pillow next to her favourite ted
Lay Jasper the cat, fast asleep in the bed.

Barbara O'Connor

How Fairy Tales End

Have you ever thought about
How fairy tales end?
If you want to find out,
Read this, I recommend.

You may have heard a story
About a dish and spoon.
They ran away from a land
With a shining golden moon.

But what they didn't tell you
Is how the tale did end.
The dish was found in pieces
And the spoon was in a bend.

A cat that played the fiddle,
A troll with a wooden club.
The troll now lives in Switzerland
And the cat plays in a pub.

Doctor Foster moved from Gloucester
Now lives in Birmingham.
He quit his job, and nowadays
He drives the local tram.

Humpty-Dumpty fixed himself
And works in cookery.
The doctor told him he'd be fine
Unless omelettes were for tea.

All these many people
Have lives beyond a book.
If you see a spider near a drainpipe
Have a closer look.

Jack Chilton (14)

Birthday Present

Bu-hu-hu and Bu-ha-ha
Are friends with Bu-hi-hi.
On a cold night
Bu-hu-hu went to see
Bu-ha-ha at his home.
He went up the street,
Turned left and
Knocked on the door.
'Who is there?'
'Bu-hu-hu!'
Bu-ha-ha opened the door
And gave a big hug to
His friend Bu-hu-hu.
'You remembered!'
'I did?'
'Yes, it's my birthday!'
'Happy birthday then.
Yes, I did remember.'
Bu-hi-hi was already there,
Eating Bu-ha-ha's big cake.
Show me your present!' said
Bu-hi-hi drinking fine orange juice.
Bu-hu-hu was already shy,
He had no present.
'Here it is!' said Bu-ha-ha,
'Friendship is the best
Present ever!'
And they all ate the big cake
And drank the fine orange juice.

Ana-Maria Mandra

The Great Debate

The Great Debate features all animals living in the towns and cities - mainly domestic animals.

The venue for this year's debate is a large empty barn near a thick forest. On the day of the event all conflicts and fights among the contestants are temporarily dropped. Even the cats are unusually patient with the rats on this day.

The topic of this year's debate is 'Dignity and Pride in the Modern Animal Culture'. The aim of the contest is to find out which domestic living thing is the least dependent on man.

'Fellow two-leg walkers, four-leg trotters, and six-leg sprinters, please listen to me,' coos a fat grey hen, who is the debate co-ordinator. 'I welcome every one of you to the most glamorous event in the animal, and insect world. Now, let the debate begin.'

A brown-looking rat with half a tail, cut by a trap, jumps on the table. 'Fellows,' it cries, 'we rats are the most wise. We do not depend on the humans for our food. Anytime we are hungry, we go to the heavily guarded human food store to steal some. We even eat from their tables at night. The humans do not feed nor groom us. Don't we have more pride than anyone here?'

Lots of applause greets the rat's defence.

A fierce-looking cat proudly mounts the table. 'The cats have more pride than the rats. We are more independent. We move alone and sometimes catch our own food. We do not walk the streets in companionship with humans as dogs do. We prefer to move alone.'

Soon, it is the turn of the domestic fowls. 'I catch flies to eat by myself,' cries the little hen. Moreover I scratch the ground and get more food for my chicks. No man does this for me. I do it for myself and my little ones.'

'Haa,' cries a goat. 'I can do without food that is provided by human beings. This is because I am very hardy and can go without food for a long time. I love looking for food on my own. I can do without man.'

'I can do without man too,' a deep voice booms from outside. A young bear jumps inside the barn and the whole barn goes silent at once. 'I have pride in my size,' the bear says. 'I get my food without anyone's help. I can even kill a man if it pleases me. I am the most independent. Don't you all agree?'

'We do, we do,' everyone chants out of fear.

'Now, we have our winner,' shouts the fat grey hen as she gives a bag of apples to the young bear.

'Good, I love apples,' says the bear as it walks away.

'Why did you give him the prize?' shouts a black goat. 'That is not fair. He isn't a domestic animal.'

The frightened hen looks at the goat. 'Why don't *you* tell him that?'

Yommie Stephen

Anna's Scottish Fairy

Once Anna lived in a beautiful house. It had roses in the front garden but she had to move away, there had been a huge fire that had demolished her father's work.

'What, I won't go! An old house in Scotland!' Anna stormed outside. Alone, running through the woods Anna started to cry. Anna didn't know what to do; if she went home she would get told off for running away.

'What are you doing?' someone asked.

'What?'

'Why are you crying?' she asked again.

'My father has to move us to Scotland, I'll freeze!' Anna explained.

'I don't know, maybe you'll like it up there,' she said innocently.

'How do you know?'

'I've friends,' she said, spreading her wings.

'Who are you? I shouldn't talk to strangers,' Anna said.

'I'm Harpeia the fairy,' Harpeia explained. 'Bye then.'

But Anna had already run part way home, she had been persuaded.

Finally they'd moved to Scotland.

'Oh how sweet!' Anna exclaimed. Anna loved Scotland.

One day Anna went for a walk in the woods.

'Hello stranger,' someone called from behind her.

'Harpeia!' Anna shouted.

'Fancy an adventure?' Harpeia asked.

'Like I didn't see that one coming!' Anna laughed.

Anna and Harpeia had many adventures, visiting other fairies and kingdoms you couldn't imagine. But those are stories for another day.

The end - or is it the beginning of a new adventure for Anna in Scottish woodlands, fields or fairy kingdoms. Anna travelled with Harpeia happily until she died.

Elizabeth Facer (13)

Bumbles' Lost Hat

Skitter, scatter, scat.
My goodness, what was that?
'It's only me,' says the bumblebee,
'I think I've lost my hat.

Can you help me find my hat?
It is my Sunday best,
I wear it with my coat and boots,
to match my stripy vest.

I'm going to a party
but I think I've lost my way.
I have a little present
to give to Dotty Gray.'

'Who is Dotty Gray?' I ask.
'Oh she is a butterfly
and I'm very sad to say
she only has one eye.

I bought her a pair of spectacles
to help her find her way,
to see the flowers in the fields
and brighten up her day.

Oh there's my hat, it's in your lap,
I thank you very much
but it's time to go or I'll be late
for the honey beer and birthday cake.'

Jenny Francis

Flight Of The Feather

It floats with style and beauty
Like the movement of a hand
The composer of the symphony
The conductor of a band

With every twist and turn the feather
Stays in balance and so light
It doesn't go against direction
It takes pleasure in the flight

Its weight will always be supported
And carried by the air
It trusts that where it needs to go
It will always take it there

Brush strokes that tell a story
Many shapes that set the scene
Of the flight it took to get there
And the places it has been

When it comes to stormy weather
With the clouds that hurry by
The flight of the feather
Paints a picture in the sky

When it seems its journey is complete
And coming to an end
The wind picks it up from where it rests
To start all over again

Matthew & Jonathan Price

Who Am I, Kids . . . ? Animal-O-Quiz

I am the biggest cat around, only in Asia to be found,
I live alone; I am active at night, I rely on my ears and excellent sight,
I have striking stripes on my coat which help me to survive,
There're fewer and fewer of me in the world, so kids, help me please! Let me stay alive!
So who am I, kids, have you guessed it yet? Of course . . . *I am a tiger!*

I am the biggest animal living on land, only in Africa and Asia to be found,
I don't look like other creatures, my trunk and tusks are my main features,
I am hunted down for my ivory, but I want to stay alive,
So kids, help me please! Do something for me to survive!
So who am I, kids, have you guessed it yet? Of course . . . *I am an elephant!*

I look funny because of my big lumps, I have them on my back, and they're called humps,
If one, I am dromedary; with two, I am a Bactrian. I travel a lot in the sand,
I live in Asia and Africa, I'm known as 'the ship of the desert', and I'm proud of it,
Even if I am strange and funny-looking, well, a bit . . .
So who am I, kids, have you guessed it yet? Of course . . . *I am a camel!*

I am an extremely interesting, although somewhat scary, creature in the world,
I am the only mammal with wings that can fly - do you know that? Have you heard?
Using voice and ears, not eyes, I can move around; everywhere in the world I can be found,
The radar was invented, just because of me, so . . . I am an important animal, surely you can see!
So who am I, kids, have you guessed it yet? Of course . . . *I am a bat!*

My strong back legs and tail help me to hop around;
On the continent of Australia I'm mainly to be found,
I carry my baby in the pouch on my belly - a safe place to be,
It's comfortable and cosy - wouldn't you agree?
So who am I, kids, have you guessed it yet? Of course . . . *I am a kangaroo!*

Anna Kroh

When Night-Time Comes Creeping

When evening comes creeping, and children are sleeping,
a whole other world starts to stir;
With moths big as house cats and hedge pigs and ding bats,
and bugaboos covered with fur!
In plasticine clotheses and noses and toeses,
the model clay gnomes all appear;
With boxes of poxes they hides under rockses,
for brewing their toadstool dew beer . . .

Then when the moon rises, up high in the skieses,
and coconut mushrooms pop out;
The elf-eating spiders with green goblin riders,
come skitting and scuttling about!
Fat pimply hobgoblins run wobblin' 'n' squabblin'
and fright things! To see how they run;
House moggies and froggies and little hedge hoggies,
chased all round the dark wood - for fun!

Until after midnight, all fierce in the starlight,
the troll and the ogre awakes;
To fill their fat bellies with small boys and jellies,
and little girls' fingers and cakes.
All clompin' and chompin' and smelly feet stompin',
they wallops and fartles and roars;
Around your house hustlin' and rustlin' and bustlin',
to snuff at your windows and doors . . .

So when night comes creeping, and you should be sleeping,
the moon's in the sky, high and bright;
Stay under the covers 'n' close to your mothers,
or you'll get a terrible fright!
For out in the darkness, not quite out of harkness,
are noises you'd rather not hear;
As scaries and hairies and one-legged fairies,
draw daringly, scaringly near!

Sullivan the Poet

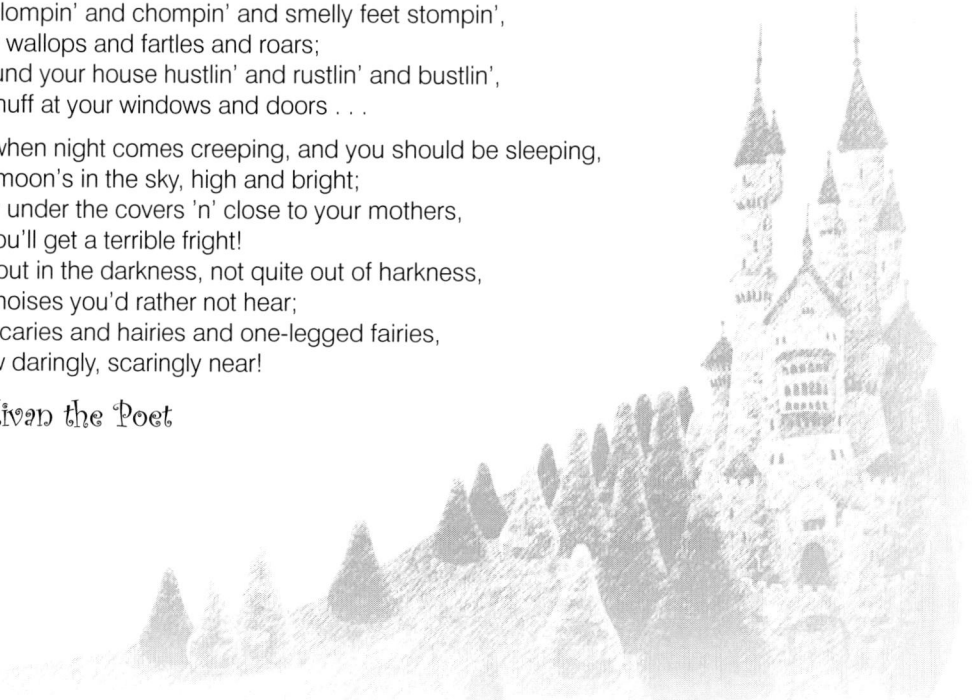

The Trip

We're off on a trip
Johnny, Mary and me,
Mum and Dad and our dog Skip,
My sister, who is only three.
On the way crisps and sweets,
Cola fizzing on my tongue,
But only as a special treat,
I really love my mum.

When we see the sea
Waiting for the train to stop,
Mary claps her hands in glee,
Johnny, spinning round like a top.
Donkeys clip-clop, their tails swish
Up and down across wet sand.
Crabs, seagulls and starfish,
Salty pebbles, in sticky hands.

Rock pools on the shore,
We paddle there, all day.
Candyfloss, ice cream galore,
Coral and seashells along the way.
A fish supper in the fading light,
Say goodbye at sunset,
Travel late, into the night,
Were we tired? You bet.

Julia Evans

My Day

When the sun goes up
       I open my eyes
          to greet the sunshine
I stretch my legs and arms
       to feel alive one more time
I do my morning exercises
       to feel strong and confident
I have my breakfast
       to wake up my senses properly

I keep on doing things which make me happy
          until I get hungry

I take my lunch to energize my body and mind

I learn and rest, I dare and test
       the world around me
It's my world as much as yours
It is a part of me and I'm a part of it
I respect it, I take care of it
       and
          in return I get lots of love
to move on in my life . . .

When the sun goes down
       I close my eyes
          to dream my sweet dreams

How's your day?

Vineta Svelch

Spider

One the wall there is a spider
making everybody scream,
for she is the creepy crawly
that can spoil a pleasant dream.

She won't harm you. She won't hurt you,
for you are far too big to eat.
All she wants is to be left
to spin her silken web so neat.

In the corner, there she climbs
between the wall and ceiling high.
Waiting for her sticky web
to catch her supper of a fly.

So stop your shouting and your squeals
for she deserves your love and hugs.
Leave her there to do what's natural
and rid you house of other bugs.

Gay Horton

Our Love

I can see sun drops warm my face
I can see snowflakes drift below
I can hear my old teddy's cries
until I reach to love him
I can feel rain sprinkle down
I can see bright colours in the sky
I can hear rainbows touch the land
until our love reaches within.

Lynne Wilson

The Big Red Balloon

I am stamping in the puddles,
From the afternoon showers.
Holding on to my red balloon,
I bend to sniff all the flowers.

A bright orange butterfly,
Brushes past and tickles my ear.
My head wobbles back and forth,
The swirling leaves I hear.

The strong wind is gusting,
Catching my big red balloon.
It pulls us high and upside down,
As I hum my favourite tune.

We fly past three seagulls,
Swooping and diving for food.
I grab a grey feather from one,
To tuck and keep in my hood.

The rumbling of a helicopter,
Turns my legs to jelly.
The spinning blades catch my balloon,
Making me drop my welly.

We dart through fluffy white clouds,
On a roller coaster ride.
The sky darkens as night draws in,
And we and the balloon collide.

The big crash pops my red balloon,
And we spiral through the stars.
Down, down, spinning and turning,
We land on my daddy's car.

Rebecca Karen Earl

Fairy Magic

Sleeping child living dreams, fairy tales' magic scenes
Like Alice and her looking glass, a fantasy through which they pass
A world of witches giving fright, flying in the dead of night
And giants with enormous feet look for children nice to eat
Boys do dream of dragons strong, mystical lands where they belong
Sailing far on pirate ship, new adventures every trip
Little girls dream of golden hair, beautiful clothes and shoes to wear
And hope one day that they will find, a handsome prince so good and kind
Watching every sleeping face, keeping dreams and magic safe
Fairies capture every heart, before the childhood years depart
For they can make all wishes real, they understand how children feel
But none have seen a fairy ring, with magic spells the wand can bring
Though unseen their life we feel, silent charms they can't conceal
Once in every hundred years, an important fairy queen appears
A blessed sleeping child is touched, with magic wand and fairy dust
Evermore enchanted days, shining aura gentle haze
Living life so brave and kind, giving others all their time
Anyone they have caressed, feels forever truly blessed

Pam O'Connor

Slug Poem

I do not like the long, moist slug
Who left a trail across my rug,
I do not like his wet, blind face,
I do not like his lack of grace.
He is Nature's darkest blot,
A living creature made from snot.

I'll get some salt to kill my foe,
He'll ooze and splutter but he'll go.
Or maybe beer will be his doom,
I'll leave a pint outside my room.
He'll squelch and guzzle, gulp and glug,
That loathsome, slimy, drunken slug.
How I'll rejoice, sing forth in praise,
When free from all his sluggish ways!

Fran Budd

Kooky Kiwi's New Home

Today is Kooky Kiwi's birthday,
he is 3 years old.
Now he is a *big* kiwi,
tomorrow Kooky will look for a home of his own.

In the morning it is bright and sunny,
Kooky listens to the birds singing.
Today he will leave home and his mum and dad,
Kooky will go and make a home of his own.

Kooky says goodbye to his mum and dad,
they say goodbye to Kooky.
He is excited but also a little sad.

By lunchtime Kooky is hot and tired,
he is very hungry too,
his bag is heavy and his ball
keeps slipping from his neck.

Suddenly! A rabbit jumps in front of Kooky.
'Hey wait!' says Kooky.
'Will you help me?
I need to find a new home.'

'Hi, my name is Carrot Top.
Have you got some lunch to share?'
'Yes I have,' says Kooky,
'Shall we have some?'

After they have eaten lunch,
Kooky tells Carrot Top what he is doing.
Carrot Top's friend Snort comes and sits on Kooky's head,
he will help too.

After a long search they find the perfect place,
trees, bushes and lovely long grass.
Here they will make Kooky's new home.

The three new friends work hard all afternoon
to make a cosy home for Kooky.
They find sticks, rocks and branches.

When it is finished it looks lovely.
Kooky is very happy, they are all very pleased with their work.
'Thank you Carrot Top and Snort!'

'Goodnight Kooky Kiwi!'

Zoë Manley

The Swan Fairy

The swan fairy sailed slowly down the river; even though she could fly she loved the gentle rhythm of the swan as it let the water help it glide through the rushes. Hidden behind its feathers she could watch the world pass her by. The children playing in the water enjoyed the sunshine and the men sitting on the riverbank with their fishing rods tried to catch the fish as they too swam quickly past.

The summer had just begun and the adventures had started when the baby cygnet was born, not one of the prettiest little ducks she had ever seen, but then she did not know that it was not a duck, because when she had found it, it had been lost and left behind when the rest of the swans had moved further down the river. It waddled like a duck, although the other ducks didn't seem to like it very much, so she stopped with it and helped it fight them off with her magic spells when they got too difficult to cope with. But as time went by they became firm friends and as he grew his colour changed and he grew and grew and went whiter and whiter until he became the most beautiful bird she had ever seen. And so she became his princess for the entire world to see and he was her carriage for all eternity.

Sheila Storr

Are You Ready To Meet Santa Claus?

Wrap up tight, Christmas is coming! The snow will get you cold and then how will you be able to wake up to see your presents. Are you ready for a white Christmas?

You can never know when Santa Claus is coming. He rides over the water, over all heights and trees just to get you the best present ever. Look outside and you will see the cushion of snow on the pavements. This is soft and cold. But remember after a long trek through all of the snow, Santa Claus needs his milk and his cookies.

You will see on Christmas Day, the moon resting on the breast of snow, it will look down on everyone below. Against the moon you may see a miniature sleigh and eight reindeer. The prancing of each little reindeer will make you jump and realise Santa Claus is on your roof. His cheeks are like roses, his beard is as white as snow and he'll shake his belly like a bowl full of jelly. You will hear him exclaim, 'Merry Christmas to all and to all a good night.'

Come now, little one, go to bed. He will seek for you wherever you are.

Tammy Samuel (14)

I Believe In God

Now I know I am still small
But in what I believe I will stand tall
I believe in God
You shouldn't be shocked or think it's odd

Mommy said God exists
Daddy said that in life there will be many twists
We all believe in God
No one should ever think it's odd

I believe in heaven up above
I believe in a blessed white dove
I know what is good and right
I know I should never get into a fight

Before I sleep I always pray
I always ask God to plan a good day
I say sorry for things done wrong
Then in my heart I feel a sweet song

Mom said God is always good
Dad said prayer is like food
I may be young but I am wise
I know that if I believe in God I will always rise

So when I feel sad and alone
There's never a need to pick up the phone
I just pray to the Lord
Then I never feel unhappy or scared

Dad said God is with me all the time
So when I pray I try to make it rhyme
God, I just want to say thank you
Please always look after Mom and Dad too.

Jessica Trappe

A Visit To Uncle Shuun

One Sunday morning
Anne went to visit her Uncle Shuun
Off she walked down to the shop of buns
It was bright, lovely and out came the sun.

Over and above the hill
She saw the farmers and the mill
After all it wasn't a big deal
Walking to Uncle Shuun's place with all will.

Once she got there,
She went in with a great care
And pampered the cute hare
And gifted her uncle with flowers in a pair.

Muzammil Sattar

Little Suzzie

Little Suzzie has an ambition
That one day she'll become an engineer with all determination
With all hard work and concentration
She will pass the examination with loads of congratulations

Little Suzzie loves scientific tools
Guided by different principles and rules
Using kilograms, grams and joules
She'd calculate and construct a pool

Little Suzzie is beautiful just like a princess with a crown
So dashing and amazing in her little white gown
Dancing all over the town
Upside down, this is not a fact but a noun.

Siddiqa Sattar

The Game's The Thing

It starts in August,
Too hot for scarves.
Taken though and trailed from cars,
Season tickets zipped in pockets.
Park the car, you must lock it.
A wall of people push their way
Towards their gate and hope the play
Will be up to snuff, or hell to pay.
Onto the pitch their heroes run,
Cool and calm in the summer sun.
'The game's afoot,' so Shakespeare said.
'Who's he play for? Oh he's dead.
Like some players,' Grandad sighs.
'We know the game is in demise.'

Come next May at the top like cream.
Top of the League.
Well, we all can dream.

Sheila Seabourne

A Snail's Words

Don't compel me
Or laugh at me,
I am always like that:
Step is short and pace slow.

My step is short and pace slow,
For my feet are short.
If you compel or laugh at me.
I will be frightened out of my wits and tumble.

You'd better let me move slowly.
Though my step is short and my pace slow,
I can reach the destination myself,
So long as I keep moving forward.

I am always like that:
Step is short and pace slow.
Don't compel
Or laugh at me.

Hsu ChiCheng

My Child

I loved you my child
Before the world began
I gave you your name
Formed you with my hand

Don't you know that I love you
That I gave myself for you
Don't you know that my Son came
And bled and died for you

I have called you by name
You are mine, precious one
I have given you life
Through the death of my Son

I will prepare a place in Heaven
So that one day you can come
And live for eternity
Giving praise to my Son

Don't you know how much I love you
That I gave myself for you
Yes it's true that my Son came
And bled and died for you.

Claire Newton

Triolet

Never lose your childish sense of wonder
At the sky when stars crystallise the night,
At the butterfly at rest on a flower.
Never lose your childish sense of wonder
At the fragile splendour of a feather,
At cobweb frosted windows in the light.
Never lose your childish sense of wonder
At the sky when stars crystallise the night.

Mary Atkinson

Mearl And Te'anara

She was part of the flowers, so proud she seemed
Her beauty a thousand men had dreamed
Dripping with dewdrops up on high
The golden sun and peerless sky
They filled with sweet enchantment her days
But her heart lay unfulfilled where're she lay
Her skin, the palest hue of gold it glowed
As if the sun its very love had showed
And when she went this way and that
The birds ached for her, flew where're she sat
Her dress was of ivy, ivory and most ancient stones
Filled with the echoes of a man's thousand moans
Grew she did, and when he came,
Her heart stood still with weary pain

'Are you lost sweet Te'anara?' were words he said
'No fair se'er, I am not lost, merely wandering like the ant from its bed
But where shall I find the sup to fill my loins
All I do is quarry and toil
It seems the Eden cannot give up its jewels to me
Or I am cursed, cursed more than another can be.'

'Sweet Te'anara, I will give you this seed
It will guide you like a faithful steed
To where your fulfilment lies
And where you will forfeit all past ties
Where your journey ends, speak the name Mearl
And there you shall find your perfect pearl
But do no more than I permit
Do not bond to him where he sits
But bring him back to your dewed domain
Or the curse will come back again
For there you will stay made out of stone
And Mearl will tear his heart out with moan
For your curse will in part move to him
And he, in part, will fade to dim.'

And so, the sweet Te'anara with her seed flew
Her heart sure of all she must do
And then she reached the whitest shores
Where the centaur Mearl hunts with mighty roars
She saw the frozen Earth, so her heart tightened
Its beauty, its grace, she ached, bidden and brightened
And when she lay on the coldest domain
Her soul became one with the diamonds of the Earth she gained

'Mearl, Mearl, come to me I seek
Let not my weary soul turn bleak
For I stand upon your frozen shores
And I hear the echo of your thousand roars
Let me fill your heart with my sweet caress
And to your heart, I kiss, I bless.'
And as she spoke, the Earth it heard
And it gave up the centaur Mearl

His hair was like raw spun gold
As ancient as a dream weaver's fold
He echoed through the mountains so vast
Where he had roamed in play till night had passed
When the two came together
The snow peeled back where they stood seemed forever
Sweet Te'anara and Mearl they saw
Their love upon high where the snow its promise bore

And there sweet Te-anara sow
Upon the flowers crushed and mixed with snow
Her seed of love for the centaur Mearl
For she had abandoned her promise of old
It grew and bore the sweetest flowers
And the sun wilted all the Earth into showers
It gave up the seed of love
And called the se'er from above
His mangled frame old from time
He threw his words down to the lovers in rhyme
'Te'anara, my life's jewel
how could you ruin, be so cruel
my toil has been laid to waste
have you forgotten our bargain, with your love's taste?
Give to me your love's seed oh Earth
And I will give it sweet rebirth
If you return but to whence you came
And never return, no never again.'

'No, old se'er these words I cannot hear
for the place of my seed is to be here
where the winter's frost breathes pink to my cheeks
and my ivy tresses with their promise leaks
send me back if you cannot gain
the seed for yourself to relieve your pain
return once more to my past lands
and make your mark again with your fair hands
for there is your true seed of love,
not mine, old se'er, not mine I say to you from above?'

The se'er glimpsed in his very soul
The ivy promise in her eyes of old
And sweet Te'anara he knew
His goddess fashioned from the morning dew
He left her there in the frozen shores
With Mearl she bore, whom she adores
And time passed on; each content
And the Earth, it filled with promises kept and un-kept
And there she slowly transformed into brown, the leaves so old
Her beauty gained from green to red, and her ivy formed her ruby bed
And Mearl the hunter of the snow, embraced her love for evermore.

Natalie Williams

Toothbrush Drill

Teeth are given to everyone a nice new set each
How to clean them regularly our parents will teach
Teeth crush our food so we can digest it with ease
When your tummy is full, your teeth are pleased
Your teeth work very hard for you so treat them right
Brush them every morning, brush them every night
Brush your teeth up and down and don't forget the back
Why not use dental floss and clean between the gaps
You must always remember the toothbrush drill
It will refresh your mouth and the germs it will kill
Every day fight the nasty germs with toothbrush and paste
Cleaning your teeth is a skill, never brush them in haste
If you neglect to brush the tooth germs away
They will discolour your teeth and make them decay
If you allow your teeth to decay, the tooth fairy will say,
'They do not deserve nice teeth, I will let them rot away.'
Treasure your teeth as the most valuable asset you have
Look after your teeth well, if you don't they will go bad
If you keep the toothbrush drill going throughout your life
People will envy your white teeth and you will look nice
Your breath will always smell nice and sweet
So if anyone wants to kiss you they are in for a real treat.

Leonard Butler

Raindrop Adventures

Roger the raindrop had grown big and plump
    as he sat in the rain cloud waiting to jump.
He wriggled and jiggled just wanting to go
    on the exciting dive to the land far below.
He was jumping so hard that he fell through and found
    he was suddenly falling alone to the ground.
'Whee-ee!' he shouted as he fell at fast pace,
    then *splat!* landed flat on a weathercock's face.
'Get off!' crowed the bird whirling like a spin drier
    and Roger was flung to the top of the spire,
then he slid down the tiles and was falling free
    when he landed *splosh* at the top of a tree.
He slid and he slithered, making the leaves laugh and dance,
    and he whispered sweet secrets to each, then, by chance,
he slipped far too fast and bounced over a twig
    and shot off to land on the ear of a pig.
He tickled the pig who shook his head hard
    and threw Roger off to land *smack* in the yard.
'Oomph,' gasped the raindrop battered and bruised, -
    then the farmer's wife trampled on him with her boots.
He clung to her heel feeling weak and thin -
    and suddenly heard voices calling to him.
When he looked up he saw falling out of the cloud
    hundreds of raindrops, a massive crowd,
all racing to join him, make puddles and pools
    for children to splash in as they charge out of school,
soak the ground so the flowers won't get too dry,
    tickle dogs so they shake and toss the drops way up high,
slide down umbrellas, splash noses, have fun,
    'til they're pulled back to the clouds by the heat of the sun.

Betty Tordoff

Cat-Astrophe!

I've lost Pumpkin-Pie, my big fat ginger cat,
she seems to have vanished and that is a fact.
I have checked all the places she usually hides,
did she get in a car and go off for a ride?
Has she fallen asleep again in with the washing,
spun in the machine and taken a squashing?
What if my neighbour, who's ever so mean,
has got her locked up so she can't have her cream?
Someone's in the bathroom now pulling the chain,
don't tell me my cat has been flushed down the drain?
The fat toad in the pond has a glint in his eye;
did he eat Pumpkin-Pie up instead of a fly?
The dog from next door has been digging around,
has he buried my ginger cat under the ground?
Perhaps she has dressed herself up in disguise,
then she could be that mouse with the little brown eyes.
She might have run off with the cat up our street,
I know Pumpkin-Pie thinks he's ever so sweet.
There were crows on the washing line pecking a vest,
have they flown off with my cat to feather their nest?
Has she climbed in a beehive to munch on some honey,
got stuck like Pooh Bear and the bees think it's funny?
Perhaps she's moved into the home of her dreams,
like a tuna fish castle with a fridge full of cream!
From way up in the tree where the plums hang in bunches,
I can hear something slurping quite loud as it munches.
With a plum in each paw, sporting bright ginger hair,
sits a fat cat that I'd recognise anywhere!
Oh, my poor Pumpkin-Pie, who put you up there?

Michele Westlake

The Lion And The Bear

The lion looked sadly through the bars
of his cage as the people passed by
and he shuddered inside at their frightened faces
whenever he let out a great sigh.
'I also feel the pain old friend,'
boomed a deep voice over his shoulder.
The lion turned to see the bear
looking back from the next enclosure.
'Just look at us,' growled the mighty bear,
'both kings of our own domains,
yet here we are, miles from home,
prisoners without the chains.'
The lion shook his great head slowly
'The bars aren't really that bad.
It's how the humans see us
that makes me feel so sad.
They're happy to let their children stroke
the donkeys, goats and sheep,
don't we deserve some of the affection
they waste on such common beasts?'
'But they fear our size and power,'
said the old bear in reply.
'To them we're just savage killers,
they don't see our gentle side.'
'But look at their children,' said the lion,
'see the small ones they push in the chairs.
They toys they hold aren't goats and sheep
but cuddly lions and bears!'

Mick Clark

The Story Of Phineas Catchpole

Phineas Catchpole is an excellent fisherman and has several trophies to prove it. He has entered a fishing competition today but so far hasn't had a single bite.

Thaddeus Toadle is also an excellent fisherman but he doesn't have any trophies to prove it. Thaddeus hasn't entered today's competition; he is determined that Phineas will not win another trophy. I wonder what he is going to do?

Thaddeus is hiding in a bed of reeds. Every time a fish swims by Phineas' line, Thaddeus slips silently into the water, grabs the fish and swallows it whole. By teatime Thaddeus is beginning to feel quite sick; but along comes another fish. Thaddeus falls into the water with a loud plop and the fish quickly swims away. Oh dear, just look at Thaddeus; he has eaten so many fish he is beginning to sink.

Back on shore Phineas feels a tug at the end of his line, and he begins to reel in his catch. Here it comes, up and out of the water. Phineas is amazed when he sees what he has caught, a very fat, very heavy Thaddeus Toadle. Phineas unhooks Thaddeus and drops him in his keep-net. When the judge comes along with his scales he announces that Thaddeus is the heaviest catch of the day and declares Phineas the winner of the competition.

Phineas goes home with another trophy to add to his collection.

Thaddeus goes home with a very sore tummy.

Mary Younger

Had To Go Hungry

He stared indignantly at his bleeding hands that were raw from chopping wood all day. He was an exceedingly dutiful and obedient monk. He couldn't believe he hadn't chopped enough wood to earn his bread and ale.

As John shuffled back to his dormitory his stomach growled. 'Ridiculous,' he muttered under his breath.

'What's ridiculous?' challenged a voice from the darker shadows along the corridor.

When John didn't reply, a figure emerged from the gloom. He had a twisted yellow face, and slits for eyes which were sunken deep into his head, a thick black sneering line for a mouth with disgustingly skeletal fingers. 'Well, well, well, had to go hungry then did we?' William cackled. 'I suppose you haven't got the muscles I have,' he taunted, flexing his stick arms under his robes. 'The ale was particularly delicious this evening, John,' he purred, licking his lips. 'Ooh! And that bread, that really was worth having,' he snarled, showing his shark teeth, that were brown, yellow and gappy. 'God clearly favours me over you!'

John, ignoring what William said, just pulled a disapproving face, as if to say, don't you know there's no talking allowed at Windystone monastery!

William was stunned John hadn't retaliated. Then he noticed John's hands and looked down at his own unscathed ones. William tossed John a hunk of bread, as he knew that John was a far better monk than he, and for once in his life felt very ashamed.

Philippa Louise Crundwell

The Deep Dark Forest

In the deep, dark forest
An eerie silence ruled.
On the forest's ferny floors
Not a creature stirred.
In the distance:
Hark the sound of hooves,
Echoing by the silent streams.
That was the sound
Of the phantom listeners
In the distance
Of the deep, dark forest,
On the ferny floor.

In the deep, dark forest
An eerie silence ruled.
A stiff wind blew,
Rustling the wispy grasses.
And the leaves of the forest stirred
As a bird flew from the turret
Of the phantom listener's house.
Alone the traveller called out loud
To the house of the phantom listeners.
Far in the distance
Of the deep, dark forest,
On the ferny floor.

In the deep, dark forest
An eerie silence ruled.
On the forest's ferny floor
Not a creature stirred.

Jocelyn Benham

Happily Ever After . . .

Once upon a time
In a nursery rhyme
Lived princesses, ogres and witches
Where little folk
Would *giants* provoke
Laughing until they were in stitches.

'Baddies' would jeer
A prince would appear
to save the lovely, troubled princess
He'd lead her by the hand
To live in a magical land
Happily ever after . . . in her beautiful sparkly dress!

Jean Holcroft

Down On The Farm

When I think of it, it makes me laugh;
The day that we drove past that field
With the cow stood in the old bath.
I bet it did nothing for her yield.

But just why did she get in there,
Did she fancy a splash about?
And I wonder if she had a care
For how the heck she might get out!

Philip Howard

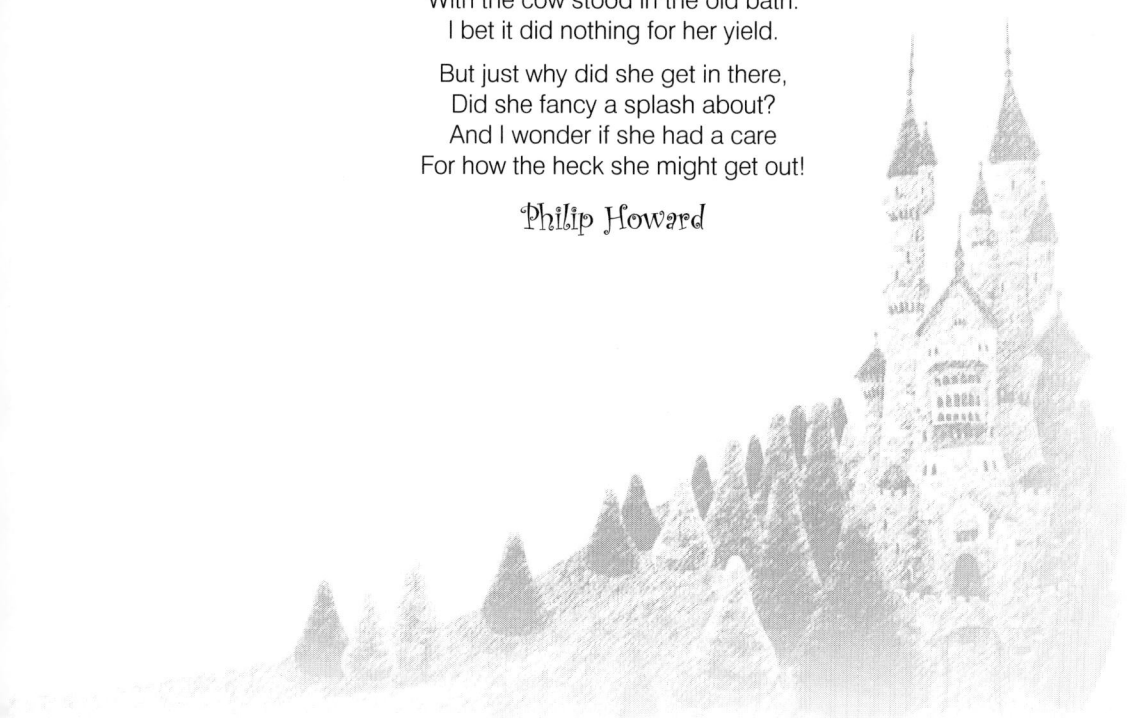

Untitled

An alien, intense, radiant glow erupted from the vial as I touched the warm red elixir and envisioned the fate of the next being that would let this nefarious liquid pass through their doomed lips. I shuddered. The concoction bubbled as I wheeled it down the corridor and into the Treehouse Ward, the children's ward. I wore a plastic smile when I arrived at the 7th bed and took a vial-full of the 'medicine' from my pocket and issued it to the worried-looking parents and an even more worried child. I then turned to walk to the exit and get my well-deserved cup of tea.

'Thank you.' I swivelled round. 'Thank you.' It was the boy.

'Only doing my job,' I said cheerily. I nearly chucked up with the guilt. Soon the child would be like the rest of them. I ran down the corridor and burst into the staff room and swallowed back a sob. I walked towards the main office and knocked.

'Come in.'

I entered, antidotes filled up the paint-stripped shelves.

'What's up?' he asked in a tone you would have never have guessed had belonged to the leader of the biggest crime organisation in the country. I walked in and grabbed the antidote before racing out. *'Get him!'* I ran down the busy corridor and smashed through the doors and issued the antidote to the children in the ward.

'Sorry, new antidote.' I smiled as I left, it was my happily ever after.

Daniel Chandler

Baxter Meets A Sunflower

Baxter, the little black poodle, was wandering around the garden. The weather wasn't particularly good, the breeze was cool and clouds were gathering in preparation for a shower, but Baxter didn't mind. He enjoyed exploring the garden and always found something new. As he had eaten all the strawberries from the strawberry patch, he made his way to the vegetable garden to look for runner beans.

'I must be careful not to pull the beans over today,' he said to himself. 'Mummy was very cross with me yesterday.'

He stood and surveyed the beans which were propped up with canes to stop them lying on the ground. There was a nice juicy bean at head height and, giving it a gentle tug with his sharp teeth, it was soon hanging from his mouth. He trotted off - to his secret patch behind the greenhouse - to eat his prize.

Lying on his tummy, chewing his bean, he noticed the large green stem of a flower swaying in the breeze beside him. He stopped chewing and looked up … and up … and up. In the sky was a large yellow flower dancing to and fro. Baxter was in awe; he had never seen such a tall flower before. Suddenly, the flower bent down, its large sun-like face against Baxter's.

'Hello,' said the flower.

Baxter was very frightened. The flower's face was covered in pimples and, as it smiled, it bared its huge teeth. Baxter didn't answer, but abandoned his bean and ran for home.

Eda Hughes

I Know A Princess

A pretty princess flying with the wind.
She skips and dances in the gardens alongside blooming bluebells.
She likes to sing to the birds.

I know a princess.
Shiny, flowery stars twinkling away
in the night sky with her today.

She is small and sweet
with a pale, pretty face
glistening with a sparkling smile,
with tiny teeth like pearls.
Long, golden, soft, loose curls and twirls cover her head
with a scent of lavender.

I know a princess.
Shiny, flowery stars twinkling away
in the night sky with her today.

A pretty princess flying with the wind.
She plays with diamonds
and is adorned with rubies,
dreams about rainbows and daisies
and shines with shining stars in the night.

I know a princess.
Shiny, flowery stars twinkling away
in the night sky with her today.

Sweet dreams princess . . .

Kiran Ali

Emma

There was once a child called Emma,
Who was sweet and gentle and good,
She was always kind to everyone,
Behaved just as a little girl should.

Now Emma had a brother called Jack,
Who was a naughty little guy,
He liked to pull her long hair hard,
Which hurt and made her cry.

But one day playing in their garden,
He slipped and fell in the mud,
His nice clean clothes were all dirty,
His knees all covered in blood.

'Oh go and fetch Mummy quickly,
Tell her I'm bleeding, I'm in pain,
Go on please Emma and I promise
I will never pull your hair again.'

So Emma ran as fast as she could
Indoors to get their mother,
Who took Jack inside, bathed his knee,
Then changed the clothes of her poor brother.

True to his word, Jack kept his promise,
Now he always treats Emma with care,
From that day to this, so I have heard,
He has never again pulled her hair.

Shirley Brooks

Peter Pan

A young boy who always
wanted to stay young to have adventure and fun
living in a place that is called Neverland.

Lived with the lost boys and Tinkerbell
but his arch enemy Hook lived there as well.

Into London Peter Pan flew
there he met Wendy, Michael and John
looking for stories to take back and tell.

Stories where good triumphs over bad
the most thrilling stories . . . that were ever heard.

All that was needed to fly
was happy thoughts and fairy dust
that lifted you into the air.

Flying off to Neverland they all went
to a tropical beautiful island
living adventures that were only in children's dreams.

Where good did triumph over bad
and other thrilling stories were heard
it was Peter Pan.

Second to the right, straight on till the morning.

Tracy

My Dog Is

My dog is
A gambolling, loveable lump

My dog is
A coat-shedding, dribbling skunk

My dog is
A smelly, old slobbering hulk

My dog is
A tail-wagging, welcoming hunk

My dog is

Angela Laws

Swingggg - The Nonsense Poem

Tumble, numble, butter, nutter,
here I come from the gutter.
Here a ding-dong, ding-dong, ding,
King Kong came with a very strong man.

Here he came knocking, bockin',
down a street without a stockin',
Tarzan and Jane came down the lane,
hit King Kong and he yelled in pain.

Chilly nilly came with Billy,
to find out what was very silly,
swhingle, swhangle, swhingle, shree,
look what's funny, King Kong's at sea.

This is the end of our swhingle, swhangle,
it's now time to go I hear the bong.
I hope we'll see you very soon,
I'm off now to fly to the moon.

Ashika Gauld

Come Little Birdie

Come little birdie, come to me,
Come little birdie from that tree.

Birdie, birdie off you fly,
All around in a beautiful sky.

Birdie, birdie in the sky,
Singing little nursery rhymes.

Hush little birdie there's no need to cry,
Mummy's come to dry your eyes.

To wrap you up and keep you warm,
Through the night from dusk till dawn.

Jenifer Ellen Austin

A Television, A Suitcase And A Hoover

I see myself as big and beautiful! OK, so I haven't got a waist, but then who does these days? No, I don't spend meal times in McDonald's.

I woke up sitting outdoors, yes it's a lovely day, but beside me I spy a television, a suitcase and a Hoover, but I can't remember how I got here. I'm feeling lonely, OK.

I don't look a pretty sight. Passers-by look at me, some shake their heads, others try to avoid eye contact. I just sit and wait . . . I don't even know what I'm waiting for.

My legs are not too good. I can't really remember where I live now. We moved recently and nobody told me my new address and if they did I probably wasn't listening, so now I'm lost and I don't recognise anyone passing by and if anyone does recognise me . . . Well, so far no one is saying.

I wish I could get up and walk . . . but, I can't.
I wish I could talk . . . but, I can't.
I wish I was back in my own room . . . but I'm not.
I wish someone would give me a hug . . . but they won't.
I wish someone would call my name . . . but I can't remember what it is.
Oh! I'm so lonely . . .

Oh, I hope it doesn't rain.

Then from distant window I hear a frantic cry,
'Where's my teddy?
I want my teddy.
I want, I want, I want . . . my big teddy.'

I want to hug myself, but I can't.

Deirdre Weir

Super Cool Big School

Samson was bursting with excitement about starting big school the following morning.

'Time for bed, you've got a big day tomorrow,' said Mum with a smile. She tucked the soft sheets around Samson's wriggling body and kissed his head.

'Mum, what will it be like at big school?' said Samson, softly.

Mum thought for a moment and said, 'It will be super.'

'Super,' said Samson, 'but how do you know, you don't go?'

'It will be super because there is a special son starting,' said Mum softly.

Samson smiled and said, 'Mum, will I like it?'

Mum sat on Samson's silver seat and said, 'Yes dear, it will be cool.'

'Cool,' said Samson, 'but how do you know, you don't go?'

'It will be cool because there is a cool, calm and collected person starting,' Mum said as she turned off the light.

'Mum, will I find it OK?' Samson said with a yawn.

Mum paused and then said, 'Yes dear, it will be big.'

'Big,' said Samson, 'but how do you know, you don't go?'

'It will be big because there is a big boy beginning,' Mum said as she walked to the door.

Samson was getting sleepy but in a quiet voice whispered, 'Will my big school be a super cool big school?'

Mum looked at Samson's long legs poking out of his blanket and smiled. 'Yes dear, and I know it will be because it's got a super cool big boy starting in the morning!'

Leonnie Mangan

Cassie At The Seaside With Gran

Cassie loved the seaside. She loved paddling in the sea and exploring the rock pools but most of all she loved making sandcastles. She had a lovely red pail and spade to match to make the sand pies.

One day her gran took her to the seaside and as soon as they were on the sand Cassie began making her sand pies. Today she was going to make the biggest castle ever.

Gran helped her to make the walls and a doorway into her castle and then Cassie made a moat right round the walls. After that she spent loads of time making sand pies which she put all round the top of the castle. It looked lovely and now Cassie had to fill the moat. She brought so many pails of water but they all soaked through the sand and Cassie was getting more and more cross. Then Gran said they would go for an ice cream and Cassie kept looking back at her lovely castle.

On their way back with their ice creams, Cassie started to run towards her castle, but where was it? She could not find it anywhere. She could see her red pail sticking up in the sand but her lovely castle had gone. Then Cassie saw that the sea was much nearer now. It was almost up to her pail. Gran had to explain to Cassie that the sea had covered her castle. They had made it too near the sea. Cassie remembered that the next time she went to the seaside!

Brenda W Craddock

A Lucky Day For An Orphan Mouse

A mouse had found herself a home in a large house. She was lonely but filled her days with games, she played her favourite, racing round and round the bottom of a pail.

One day a face peered at her. She cowered low, but a kindly voice asked, 'What are you doing Miss Mouse? Your life is in danger, the owners do not like any animals. Do not be afraid, you must come home with me.' She plucked up the mouse and put her into her work bag.

The cleaning lady hurried her work and raced home. She kept a room for all the rescued animals she found but didn't have another mouse. She gently placed Coffee in a glass tank. 'I've named you Coffee because you're brown and cream. Is that fine with you?'

'Oh yes! It's lovely to be named.'

'This week I'll buy you a friend, the same colouring, then you'll look like sisters.'

Sue kept her word, a warm-hearted lady. 'This is Toffee,' she said before placing her in the glass tank beside her rescued mouse, Coffee. 'Once I'm sure you are good friends, you can be together.'

One morning Sue couldn't find Toffee, her tank was empty. She felt inside her nest, out scampered a baby mouse Eeny, another Meeny, followed by Miney and Mo. What a surprise! Toffee was expecting babies at the shop. Now Coffee had five new friends. Wow! What happiness!

Hilary Jill Robson

Old Mrs Spider

A flighty young fly got caught in a web,
'My supper,' smiled old Mrs Spider,
'This blackberry bush is a fine place to be,'
And she wove her web wider and wider.

'You're a nice fat prize,' she said with delight,
'And my scheme you have to admire,
Flies like blackberries and I like flies,'
And she wound her web higher and higher.

'You let me go,' cried the frightened young fly,
Adding, 'please,' which is much politer,
But sly Mrs Spider just licked her lips
And twined the threads tighter and tighter.

Then the sky grew dark and the rain poured down
And the wind blew mightier and mightier,
A blackberry dropped, and plopped right through the web
As the lightning flashed brighter and brighter.

Old Mrs Spider clung to a leaf
With her torn web tattered beside her,
And the fly winked his eye, as he waved her goodbye,
'No supper tonight, Mrs Spider.'

Gina Claye

There's A Mouse In My Shoe

There's a mouse in my shoe!
Whatever shall I do?
I let out a shriek, it replies with a *squeak,*
scurrying back down to the toe.

My stubborn little friend,
no more time will you spend
making your home in my shoe.
Now hurry along as I have lots to do!

Beady black eyes, shiny and bright,
soft little paws, velvet and white,
long satin tail you flick with delight,
please, please get out of my shoe!

School starts very soon,
I'm going to be late,
oh, don't make me wait,
please get out of my shoe!

What a *squeak* and a scurry, you dash in a hurry
to my doll's house to make a new home,
stay as long as you like, snuggle up and sleep tight
and thank you for getting out of my shoe!

Emma Stoffer

If I Was . . .

If I was Superman
I would never need to be Batman
If I was the prime minister
I would always visit Winchester
If I was the Queen
I would ensure the city streets were clean
If I was a teacher
I would turn the children into many a preacher
If I was a doctor
I would thoroughly check her
If I was a television reporter
I would need a stool to make me taller
If I was a religious leader
I would teach the religious faiths to every reader
If I was a lollipop woman
I would emphasise how we are all human
If I was an astronaut
I would end up in court, for astronomy I have not been taught
If I was a police officer
I would have to arrest her
If I was a judge
I would from my final decision not budge
If I was a cleaner
I would make windows and doors shinier
If I was what I want to be
I would live my life happily and contentedly.

Ramandeep Kaur

Big Ambitions

Alan was an elephant,
There's no denying that.
He had a trunk, he had some tusks,
The Earth shook when he sat.

He longed to be an actor,
He had not other goals,
But was wary of being typecast
In the elephant based roles.

So he practised method acting
And he learnt to dance and sing,
In the hope they'd see that he could turn
His hand to anything.

But alas, it was to no avail,
The directors and the rest
Could only see an elephant
As scenery at best.

But Alan's not a quitter
And he took work where he could,
He's a film out in November,
The reviews are rather good.

Perhaps some day he'll be a star,
When he's a little older,
But for now he's really quite content
To play a big grey boulder.

Edward Harris

Trying To Write A Story

Downstairs the clocks are ticking
Sitting happily on the wall,
Upstairs by my desk
I am feeling such a fool.

Trying to write a story,
One that nicely flows,
One word or another,
Nothing really goes.

When I write on the page,
It sounds like someone else's,
Like another person's story,
I really cannot help it.

A different person's words
Copied out by me,
Same appearance,
Different personality.

When I am a little older
I will write with words my own,
Unlike a story I once started,
The story of the forgotten bone.

Jessica Underwood (13)

War Time Teddy Bear

Monty was an odd-looking bear
Whose nose was squashed and flat
His trouser button eyes were spaced far too wide
You wondered who he was looking at!
His body was round and made of pyjama cloth
Sausage arms and legs dangled on each corner end
With stuffing of kapok
He cost ten shillings from the shop;
My brother's faithful old war time friend.

Jenny Fensom

I'm Next Door To An . . .

I'm next door to an . . .
Ogre - and I don't like it.

He wants to specify
my every move.
He calculates
without question: how much
I weigh, what I eat, when.

He wants to absorb me -
liquid, lump, loose 'til
I weep for the vacuum
he's created for the sun.

In this black hole
I'll hide - I'll bide,
brood and deep twist truth -
until an emancipated stride

a sudden surge of strength
will rise, a morning sun.
I'll get him back!

The trees abound with birds,
encourage me, charge me.
Call to me with stories

of grass on hillsides. Stars over
other worlds, flowers as big
as arms can stretch!

The Ogre hungry, he's out to stalk!
Sticks and stones, he's so large . . . I'm so alone . . .

Consequences Ogre!
A snap of fingers, a release of energy . . . A crack of laughter!
The Ogre's melted into stickable plaster! *Ha, ha, ha, ha, ha!*

Rosalind Lee

Miggle-Muffin

Strange name, yes, that's right, Miggle-Muffin!
Think, before you switch off that light,
Its smiley face is o' so wrong,
Its curly tongue so very long,
To lick around the room for liars,
It knows if you've been lighting fires,
It senses if you've fought or stole,
And if you have, you'll pay the toll!
The creature's out there, below the ground,
Where the grass is bumpy, lumpy, round,
It's special, as it sees your wrongs,
It comes at night to sing its song,
And from its mouth, 'Migg, Migg,
I'm here, are you bad? If so then fear.'
Until you wake, you'll see no change,
Then if it got you, things turn strange,
Accidents, illness, and awful flu,
Temperature, headaches, vilest spew,
You will suffer and have no play,
The most miserable putrid sickest day,
Or, if you were really bad,
Days and days you'll be so sad,
Wait, did you hear that thud?
But don't worry if you've been good,
So take heed, it's close, nearby,
No one to save you from your cry,
Just you, and your good nature too,
Now, when I switch that light off,
Will it come for you?

Stuart Braggs

If Potter Lost The Battle

What if Harry Potter had died
And Lord Voldemort ruled all?
The Weasleys would have wept
While the Death Eaters had a ball.

Poor Hagrid would have been bereft,
Sobbing hard into his beard,
Watched with cruel amusement by 'He
Who Must Not Be Named', just feared.

Hermione would have been enslaved
With the other mudbloods, themselves
Reduced to being treated worse
Than any poor house-elves.

The Dark Lord's followers baying for
Blood-traitors like the Weasley clan
To be rounded up and carted off
To cold and spooky Azkaban.

Ron, dreading the dementor's kiss
As much as Lavender Brown's,
Giving his family extra wands
To hide beneath their gowns.

Hogwarts would never be the same,
Slytherin the only house,
Gryffindor Tower closed down
And Peeves quiet as a mouse.

No, Harry Potter cannot die!
And the Dark Lord mustn't rule.
He'll soon regret picking a fight
At Hogwart's Wizarding School.

Tracy Davidson

Cosy Rain

If it would rain,
each and every day,
I would be a very happy girl -
I say.
Happy as can be
from the water that I see.
From the pitter-patter raindrops
falling down on me.

I love the cosy feeling
of listening as rain hits the ceiling.
While I'm in my nice, warm house
there's thunder and lightning outside scaring the mouse.
I'm snuggled up.
I feel so fuzzy and warm.
this is the feeling -
I want to wake up to every day at dawn.

Many people reprimand me
and tell me I'm insane.
A lover of the rain? They exclaim -
is really rather strange!
I do feel sad and disheartened -
that many are not like me,
enjoying the rain
and feeling its tranquillity.
I guess I'm rather odd -
I even like Marmite with Cod!
But everyone is different I guess
we can't be the same
to me, that would certainly be insane!

R. Al-Jassar

The Dippy Tippohotamus

My friend the Tippohotamus
All come his words out wrong.
He can't remember simple rhymes
Or all the words of songs.

So well he never does at school
Although he tries to please.
I think he's broken every rule
And most of these with ease.

My friend the Tippohotamus
His shoes are always wrong.
His left one seems to fit his right
His laces never done.

Our class went on a summer trip
And trip is what poor Dippy did.
He landed on a flower stall
Which smashed against a red brick wall.

Our teacher quickly stopped and stared
With roses clinging to her hair.
The only thing she found to say
Was, 'Not another Dippy Day.'

The Dippy Tippohotamus
I wished he'd find his way
And find his way is what he did
He did it yesterday.

For yesterday in swimming class
Our teacher set us all a task
And Dippy proved he was the best
At underwater holding breath.

Stephen Skivington

Fun At The Fair

The fair is here, it's the time of the year
The children all love it and they do cheer
Candyfloss light as air
So, so sticky but nobody cares
Popcorn crackling, the smell a delight
Hot dogs a-plenty, they taste all right
Goldfish in bowls, swimming round and round
Hoping to win one, plastic bags to be found
Bells are ringing and shrieks of glee
Children laughing, enjoyment to see
Chairoplanes swinging high up in the air
What fun to be up there looking down at the fair
Bingo's in full swing, a winner or two
A glass plate or vase, the colour of blue
The man at the stalls shouts, 'Do try your luck
Roll up, roll up, you might win a duck.'
The children just love it and adults too
The fun of the fair is all there for you.

Sheila MacDonald

The Pirate

The pirate came with a terrible roar
With a sword and a cutlass to our front door

He'd a red scarf knotted around his neck
And a bobbing parrot that went peck, peck

'Come in,' said Mum, 'take a break from the sea
Cause even a pirate needs his tea.'

Sheena Blackhall

The Zoo

The parrots are talking on a big tamarind tree,
A big harpy eagle blinking her round eyes at me.
The old lion is resting in his iron cage,
My daughter, Rachel, is drawing his face on a page.
A big crocodile in a pond pushes up his head to breathe some air,
My son, Daniel, running away in fear.
My wife feeds a lovely deer with green leaves,
Children are playing with the monkeys in the trees.
A huge elephant grumbling in the rain,
A lonely snake crying in a shallow drain.
A hungry tiger searching for a piece of meat,
Birds are shouting in the sun's boiling heat.
The fat water cow rejoiced in his swallow mud house,
A ravenous bush cat chasing at a very busy mouse.
Hungry baboons dancing in their cages happily,
A green macaw sings upon a coconut tree merrily.
Lazy snakes are climbing on top of a naked tree,
A hungry anteater nibbling at a dead honeybee.
A flock of birds singing and clapping at me.
I wonder at their voices and their beautiful melody,
The zoo is the best place my family and I can be,
That's an animal paradise my children love to see.

Gideon Cecil

Secret Gardening

Secrets are a hidden thing, all lost and there to seek
The garden has been spoken of, so all now want a peek
The stories of its treasures, sink deep into the mind
Until no more, we simply must adventure, seek and find!

Adventure starts upon the gate, please tell of what you see
It's overgrown and thick with green, I cannot see beyond . . .
Shall we venture through and past this wretched ivy growth?
Yes, oh yes, oh please we must, but first the magic key!

It clunks and creaks and opens slow, and then all falls so quiet
Once parted wide, and stood beyond, the ivy slow reveals
A sight and smell and sound to all that opens senses wide
Slow venture well beyond the gate, reveals what's deep inside.

Each glance allows the eyes to fill with new each time they stare
Each breath inhale engulfs with air of sweet and fragrant smells
Each sound requires more venture to seek and find its source
Each touch reveals a texture new, and gentle but of course

And though the steps have yet been few, a taste they do provide
To venture far and deep within, to find what else does hide
No venture one, or two, or three, will ever reveal my all to thee
So do return to play again, my pathways will be kind
Remember me, and tell no soul, for then I'm there to find
And the secret is the *key* to this, so turn it as you leave!

Andrew Pickersgill

Milo The Giant

Milo the giant was incredibly tall,
his shoes didn't fit and his coat was too small,
he couldn't do much because of his height,
to see him, his size, was an awesome sight.
But it wasn't much fun being this high,
constantly stared at, as people went by.
He never went out, or played in the park,
just sit all alone, at home in the dark,
frightened and scared what people would say,
when all that he wanted was friends that would play.
When you're as tall as the tallest giraffe,
it isn't much fun, you can't have a laugh,
no one can hear, you're having to shout,
this is what being a giant's about.
He couldn't ride a bike, or sit in a car,
sit in a plane, or go very far.
Life seemed boring, with not much to do,
with not much to fit him, with games so few.
But Milo seemed happy, and really sincere,
the same time, the same month and same time of year,
despite the problems his tallness could be,
he would always decorate the town Christmas tree.

Jonathan Rhodes

The Sleigh With Go Faster Stripes

He sets his alarm for a quarter past twelve
But just before midnight he is awoken by elves
The sleigh is packed and the reindeer are steady
The harness is polished and everything's ready

Months of hard work by an army of friends
The manufacture of toys to satisfy trends
Computers and footballs and video games
Together with old favourites with more traditional names

The red sleigh with go faster stripes is packed to the brim
With holly and mistletoe perimeter trim
It hurtles into the sky at the speed of sound
Leaving behind it a flurry of snow on the ground

Onward and onward into the night
In the distance dancing the northern lights
Skimming across treetops and frozen lakes
Driving through snowstorms if that's what it takes

He mustn't be late and his work must be done
Before Christmas daybreak has finally begun
Landing on rooftops, parking in gear
Sliding down chimneys full of good cheer

Tip-e-toeing to the tree in the centre of the lounge
Hastily placing presents whilst glancing around
Nibbling at mince pies and sipping mull wine
Suddenly realising he hasn't much time

With a finger of magic touching his nose
Up the chimney at breathtaking speed he goes
His reindeer are waiting, raring to go
He jumps in his sleigh and is off with a high-ho

Repeating his action a million or more times
Following his route crossing off line by line
Weary and fatigued he soldiers on and on
He must finish every household, he doesn't have long

The crimson horizon has started to appear
The last house is finished and he gives a big cheer
He shouts merry Christmas and a happy new year
And wishes all good children love and peace without any fear

Clive Atkins

Toys 4 US Means 'Happily Ever After'

Rocking horse, rocking horse,
where will you take us today?
Will it be to Fairyland
to stay all day and play?
Will it be to Timbuctoo
or here at home to stay?
Rocking horse, rocking horse,
nod your head and neigh.

Hobby-horse, hobby-horse,
let's go for a run
up and down the passageway,
it really is such fun
pretending we can gallop
or proudly trot along.
Hobby-horse, hobby-horse,
let's sing a riding song.

Teddy bear, oh Teddy bear,
will you bring your friends
to share a picnic with us,
have fun that never ends?
We've got a special tea set
of yellow, blue and red.
Teddy bear, oh Teddy bear,
let's have a cuddle instead.

Zzzz . . . sshhh . . . it's Happily Ever After Land,
the land of wishes and dreams
where we can go wherever we want,
pretend life's not what it seems;
It's a place where fun time never stops
and dreams go on forever
in Happily Ever After Land
where all our toys are clever.

Ann Voaden

The Other World

Vance and Pelagia ran in to their back garden, on a day that was splendid with crisp sunshine and friendly blue sky with the sweetest clouds. They wanted to water the flowers that were such a sea of colours and textures.

'Mum's going to love it when she finds out we've done the watering,' said Pelagia to her older brother. 'She likes it when we're useful!'

'She did the last time we got busy with the flowers,' said Vance smiling and trying to picture their happy mother.

Suddenly, after a brilliant flash of silver light, a tunnel appeared in the garden. The two children looked at each other, then decided to enter it.

They walked for a while, surrounded by a deep silence, in a tunnel of white light. They emerged out the other end in a world of rainbow colours, pleasant sunlight and breeze.

'I love it here, I don't want to go back,' said Vance leaping about in joy.

'Me too,' said a happy Pelagia. 'It's so lovely here.'

They spent hours exploring the flowers and meadows, lakes and waterfalls. But when darkness fell they heard strange hisses and ghostly sounds, and ran.

'Quick, we have to reach the tunnel,' shouted Vance to a frightened Pelagia. They looked around to see dark beasts and ghostly demons chasing them.

When the two children got back home, they were more than relieved. And later, they were overjoyed to see their mum and dad.

Muhammad Khurram Salim

Cat And Mouse

His whiskers twitched as he tested his surroundings for safety before scampering up the nearest gladioli stem. Along the garden path, paved and pebbled neatly, came Jonathan; clogs clattering loudly on the stones as he bounced a bright yellow ball in front of him; totally unaware of the tiny mouse now hiding among the pink flowers of the gladioli. Horror of horrors, behind him followed his younger sister Emily; Emily of the incessant chatter and bobbing ringlets. Tommy Mouse didn't like her much. She had a cat called Tiger and he didn't like that either - it always tried to catch him. Wherever Emily was, he knew, the cat wouldn't be far away.

Tommy began to shiver with fear, causing the golden yellow pollen from the nearest flowers to sprinkle all over him. He sneezed. The sound was tiny … but Emily chose to be silent at that very moment and Jonathan heard it. Curious, he began to search through the flowers until he came eye to eye with Tommy. They gazed at each other. Jonathan grinned - a grin of pure evil. Without looking behind him, he said, 'Here, pussy, pussy, here's your dinner.'

But Tommy wasn't about to become anyone's dinner. Like a monkey in the jungle, he almost flew from flower to flower, making a complete getaway. He knew that cats don't like water, so paddled on a large leaf to the centre of the pond. There he rested, smiling to himself because he had beaten Tiger and now was safe.

Pat Spear

Little Ladybird

Sitting in the garden the other day
A ladybird landed on me, I think it wanted to stay
It crawled up and down my arm then onto my back
I thought, *no little ladybird*
I've had enough of that
So I picked it up carefully, I didn't hurt it at all
Because ladybirds are lovely and they are very small
I then put it on the grass
And thought, *you will be happy there*
But it wasn't long before
It was climbing back up my chair
Later I went inside to make myself a drink
Guess what I saw upon my kitchen sink?
The little ladybird was there
It must have come in on my clothes
How fast it got there nobody knows.

Margaret Holyman

I Wish I Was A Bat

I wish I was a bat
Flying around at night
I'd terrify the cat
And give the dog a fright

I'd hang upside down
I wouldn't sleep in a bed
But do you think my nightgown
Would fall over my head?

Liz Holt

Bootboy

'Don't put that foot inside me!'
Cried Football Boot to Sock.
'It's okay muddy or grassy
But not farmyard smells of livestock!'

'I don't want to play with you!'
Tackled Sock in quick retort.
'The coach selects, I haven't a view -
My sweet advice is never sought!

Why Boot do you always whine?
They think you're cute with your lace!'
'Put a sock in it, toe the line!'
Mouthed big Boot, 'or I'll kick yer face!'

'Foul!' yelled Sock, 'you're highly strung
And are always so uptight!
When you have learned to hold that tongue,
Use your eyes to gain more insight!'

Boot screamed back, 'I'm a twelve size,
An important part of the kit!
At last I'm not held up with ties,
Nor am I plain or purl, you nit!'

'Le' go,' sobbed Sock, 'you're a heel!
Go, stub your toe, mudslinger!
And miss your shot - that's how I feel -
You're a soulless, screwed up winger!'

Bob Crittenden

The Wee Fairy On Top Of The Christmas Tree

The wee fairy on top of the Christmas tree
Was feeling somewhat lacklustre and jaded.
Her tinsel crown had slipped over one blue eye,
And her glittering gown had become faded.

Christmas was fast approaching and snow falling,
And sounds of Santa Claus' bells were heard tinkling
As he made to all his seasonal calling;
How could she face Santa no longer twinkling?

But Santa's gaze fell on her as he landed
In the grate, red-suited and blue eyes winking.
He quickly saw the fairy's situation
And, aware of her plight, it set him thinking!

He dug in his pocket and pulled out star-dust
Which he had captured whilst on his long journey.
He blew the dust gently in her direction
And whispered magic words over the fairy.

There was a sudden bright flash of starry light
And there upon the tree she hung all afire.
Her sparkle had returned with a fine new gown
And stars hung round her head as a tiara.

Santa Claus beamed and swept into a low bow,
Then with his reindeer flew off in the night
To complete this his yearly Christmas journey,
Leaving the fairy in a state of delight.

She preened and pouted in the dark of the night,
This eve of Christmas she softly glowed with peace.
When the family awake she will shine bright
For them as they celebrate this festive feast.

Gwendoline Douglas

Two Little Twins

Samuel and Jack are four-year-old twins
They share their toys and eat nice things
They go to school and have fun every day
And love building sandcastles on holiday

Sometimes they are brave and sometimes sad
That's when they look to their mum and dad
To the dentist, optician and doctors they go
Brave little soldiers then away they go

They love kicking leaves and climbing up trees
And rolling in mud to get dirty knees
And sledging in snow is so much fun
But mostly they love to play safe in the sun

They help to recycle bottles, card and tin
And help pick up litter to put in the bin
They love to play with their friends in the park
But don't stay out after it's dark

Hayley Huttlestone

Happily Ever After

Can't wait for the snow
I waited and waited
Then it came
With all its whiteness
And all its greatness
With lots of snowflakes
I made a snowman
Sat near the fire
Watched TV
Feeling warm and safe
With all my family
Happily ever after.

Sarah Abdelbaset (9)

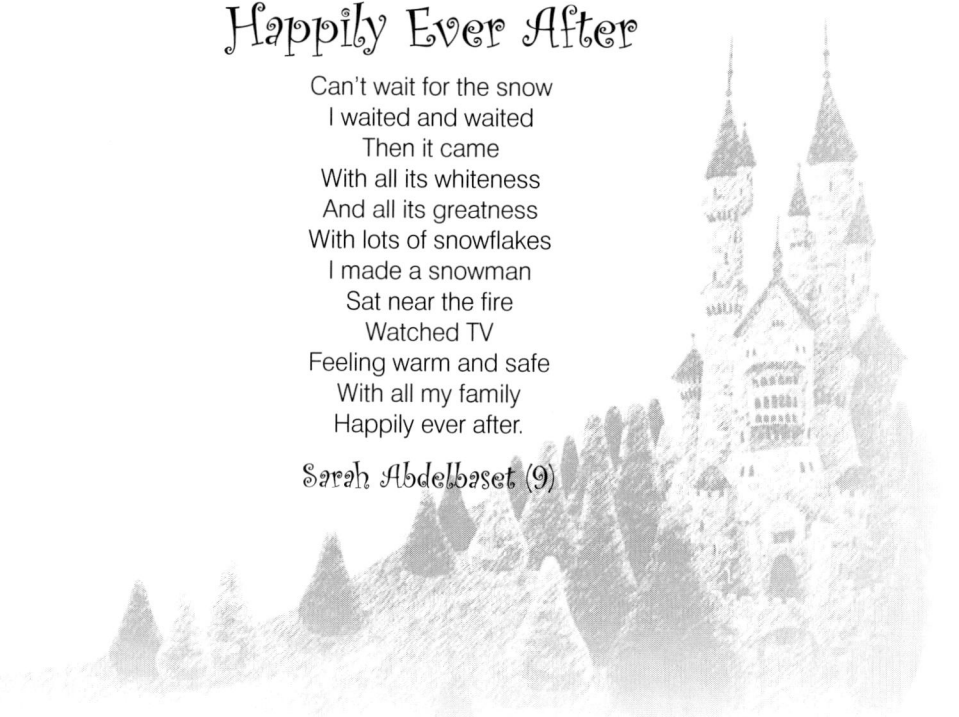

Tomorrow's Play

'Mam, can I go to the woods tomorrow?'
'Ah, the woods. Well, we'll see.'
We'll see! We'll see!
I mean, where does that leave me?

I want to go to the woods!
To run and play among the trees,
Maybe pick some bluebells for Mum,
That ought to please.

Why can't I go to the woods?
A simple, 'Yes,' or, 'No,' would do.
Well actually no. I want a, 'Yes.'
But, 'We'll see. We'll see.'

What's there to see?
The gang will probably be there
And we'll have some fun. Yeah!
I expect we'll play escape and evade

Yeah! I'll hide down by the fallen beech,
Where all those brambles are.
Even their long sticks won't reach . . .
'Oh Mam! I want to go to the woods!'

J G Ryder

The Light Warrior

Sitting upon his steed,
Brave and strong,
Bedecked in armour,
And bestowed in honour,
Innocents he has freed,
From the evil-doers of wrong,
A maiden's lover,
He'd do anything for her.

A story goes,
Once his girl was kidnapped,
By a Duke of ill repute,
An army stood before him,
Upon the fortress our gallant knight blows,
To save his lady who was trapped,
One swing of his sword he killed the brute,
Our warrior took his maid home to be safe within.

If ever there is danger,
If ever there is peril,
The Light Warrior,
And more of his kin,
Will save a baby for its manger,
Combat any unruly ill will,
The Light Warrior,
Has the power to crush all sin.

Jonathan Simms

The Beginning Of The Wanders –
A Fantasy Tale
(Not for children to try doing themselves)

Ten-year-old Anne was delighting in gathering primroses and marvelling at the luxuriant moss which was growing on the large stones which were scattered around. Anne was so engrossed that she didn't realise that she was getting deeper into the dell and it was becoming forest. Suddenly, Anne realised that the bright sunshine had gone and it was quite dim. She found herself surrounded by tall trees with hanging creepers. As she looked up, an amazing thing happened, a being like a man but of an ethereal quality and totally golden and glittering, stepped down from the air.

This marvellous being spoke to Anne saying, 'I am the Primrose Prince and also the Wanderer of the World.'

In childish innocence she replied, 'Oh, I'm delighted to meet you, Primrose Prince. My name is Anne and I would like to wander the world,'

'You shall my dear,' he replied, 'you have been given the gift of being able to see me. Most people cannot see me. If you touch the hem of my coat, most people will not be able to see you either. Also, when we will go on trips around the world, it will seem a long time but in reality it will only take a few seconds.'

Anne touched Prince's hem and immediately they were flying high.

Caroline A Carson

Saving Stick The Scarecrow

Stick the Scarecrow, who lived in the orchard, was very sad and Cherry B, the fruit fairy, dried his tears with her wings.

'The farmer is going to throw me over the hedge and I shall become just a pile of twigs again,' sobbed Stick.

'All because I cannot frighten the birds and they eat all the fruit in the orchard.'

Cherry B tried to comfort Stick. 'This is because they love you. They love fluttering along your long arms and on top of your green hat for their morning chorus and taking your straw hair for their nests.'

Stick's tears finally stopped and he fell fast asleep but for Cherry B and the fruit fairies, work was about to begin!

Next morning, and every morning, the wooden bird table was covered with warm butterfly cakes which Cherry B and the fruit fairies had made during the night.

The garden birds spotted the cakes at once. They ate so many, they were too heavy to fly into the fruit trees. So, all the apples, plums and pears grew rosy and ripe in the summer sunshine.

The farmer was very pleased indeed and, as autumn turned towards winter, he put Stick into an old leather armchair in the garden shed. Cherry B and the fruit fairies were already there, baking lots of cakes and making delicious rose petal tea. Everyone inside the garden shed would be cosy and warm this winter, while outside, the land silently became covered in snow.

Maggie-Amelia Nixon

An Animal Anomaly

I'm a green frog, a lean frog, a preen frog - I'm vain!
I'm a creep frog, a leap-frog, a sleep frog, just plain;
I'm a lump frog, a plump frog, a jump frog in the rain;
I'm a wet frog, a jet frog swimming in the drain.

I'm a gad fly, a mad fly on the window pane,
A blue fly, a new fly riding on a train,
A dad fly, a glad fly a-singing this refrain,
A shy fly, a high fly climbing up a crane.

I'm a red bug, a bed bug - a dead bug under you,
A short bug, a fraught bug squashed inside a shoe,
A small bug, a crawl bug, a bug without a clue,
A humbug, a mum bug, a mother loyal and true.

I'm a goldfish, an old fish, a bold fish in a bowl,
A catfish, a fat fish, looking rather droll,
A quick fish, a slick fish, a trick fish in a shoal,
A chic fish, a geek fish, a clique fish: I'm a sole.

I'm a dry snake, a sly snake, slithering through the grass,
A smart snake, a dark snake: quick, just let me passss . . . !
A cool snake, a cruel snake - my eyes are like cut glass,
A rattlesnake, a battlesnake: they say I am 'first class'.

So you see how we are free ones - we cannot be your pet;
We won't let you examine us: we've never met a vet.
You can't snatch or catch us in a cage, nor with a net:
We'd disappear and laugh at you. *That* you may safely bet!

Katharine Holmstrom

Henry And The Tooth Fairy

Under the pillow goes the broken tooth in the hope of financial reward.
It took so long to loosen and pull, this had never happened before.
It's quite a serious business as a tooth could be worth quite a lot.
For the one he pulled last Sunday, a pound was what he got.

Life isn't always easy 'cause there are sweets and comics to buy.
So even though it was half a tooth, it must surely be worth a try.
In the morning he woke quite early and under his pillow he found
A pound coin all new and shiny and he hadn't heard a sound.

Then next to the money he noticed a paper with writing in gold.
It was simply addressed 'To Henry' with words that were large and bold.
'Dear Henry', the letter started, 'I'm the fairy that brings you the cash,
There'll be no more nocturnal money; this time is definitely the last.

I don't need any more tooth stumps; my cupboards are full to the top.
You'll have to do chores for your Mummy, I'm sure she'll pay you a lot'.
Henry was so disappointed; he wrote a reply straight away,
'Dear fairy', his small hand was shaking, 'Please listen to what I've to say.

It's Mummy's birthday next Sunday and I'm saving to buy her a gift.
There's no one to give me the money, 'cause there's only Mum and me left'.
When the fairy found Henry's letter it brought a tear to her eye.
She decided to make Mum a present, so that Henry needn't buy.

The gift was left 'neath his pillow, wrapped in gold coloured gossamer hair,
And inside was something so precious, a pearl for his mother to wear.
It was made from the dust left from wishes that fairies would sprinkle at night
And glued together with magic that shone on the darkest night.

Henry gave her the gift on her birthday, he was such a proud little boy.
She looked at the gift in amazement her eyes filled with tears of joy.
But the secret they'd soon discover was the pearl, so shiny and new
Was filled with magical powers that made all their wishes come true.

Lynne Tippett

Stars, Moon, Dark And Shadow

The stars come out each
night for you,
And the moon, and the
dark, and the shadows too.

The stars await your
whispered wish,
They shine of your hopes,
each star you notice.

The moon awaits your
dreamy gaze,
It glows of elegance,
all night it stays.

The dark awaits your
curtains drawn,
So it can live
before the dawn.

The shadows await your
final task,
As trees will admire
the shapes they cast.

Rebecca Mummery

Bunny's Big Adventure

I thought I was unique
Just one of a kind,
Destined to be lonely,
On nobody's mind,
That is, until today,
When I was taken out
To meet some furry friends
Who greeted me with a shout!
There were bears and mice,
Dogs and cats, and bunnies,
That was especially nice,
Because now I have a family
Aunts and uncles, cousins too,
All made me feel so welcome,
Better than visiting a zoo,
We played games on the lawn
And had a picnic tea,
Little ones began to yawn,
It had been a hectic day,
The sun was slowly setting
As I was getting ready
With many paws a-waving
And a chorus, pitched, unsteady,
They were all a-saying
   'Come back, and see us soon!'

Jackie Domingo

Outmoded

When grannies get together
they mutter and mumble
you don't know whether
they'll utter praise or grumble
if they knit their brows
clench their teeth and frown
it could be your blouse
that gets a dressing down
if they start to flap
squeal and clap
their hands with glee
then it's for certain
you're dressed in a curtain
that they think is pretty
but when they start to say
'You know in my day,'
or, 'When I was a girl,'
and your toes curl
with embarrassment
it's because you're not meant
to look so grown-up
so to avoid being shown up
by your dear old nan
be as young and sweet as you can
I know it is really absurd
but grannies do not believe in
being seen and not heard!

Sonia Singer

Fiery Tigers' Tails

I chase fiery tigers' tails,
Sometimes they burn my fingers.
I cool my fingers in turquoise waters
While the emerald jewels of the lake
Wink at my reflection.

Fiery tigers they have fiery tails
And are longer than my dad.
They fly across wide open skies
Like fireworks, then sneak off into space.

Fiery tigers like to call my name,
They invite me out to fly.
In the sky my feet twist and turn,
In the wind my hands twist and shake
As I rocket across the evening sky.

By night-time I've grown tired
Of chasing fiery tigers' tails.
So I sleep on the desert floor.
A desert fox keeps the wind from me.
Stars become my bedtime light.

When I sleep I dream of fiery tigers,
They sing and dance to tempt me,
But in my dreams I can fly,
So I chase fiery tigers across the sky.

I chase them till the ends of space,
Where a million tigers are running,
Their long fiery tigers' tails light up
The edges of the universe,
As they endlessly eat into outer space.

David Swan

Jim

There once was a man named Jim,
Who wanted to go to the gym.
He went to the shop,
Bought some fizzy pop,
And then met his friend called Kim.

And so he then went to her flat,
Where he lay down on a mat.
As he twisted the top
He knocked over the pop
And Kim cleaned it up with a mop.

They went on a trip to the zoo,
He looked at a yak that said moo!
A cheeky monkey jumped on his back,
And Jim nearly had a heart attack.

So when he went back to Kim's flat,
He got a fright from her black cat
Because it had jumped on his back.
Jim said, 'What's this on me?'
And Kim simply said, 'That's Jack.'

Kim told Jim she was going for a workout,
'I'll come with you!' Jim said in a shout.
As they walked down the street,
Jim felt excitement right up from his feet,
At the words 'There it is' said by Kim,
He finally got to the gym.

John Alexander Wallace

The Rose Fairy

(For Linda and Lynne, and my little niece Rosie)

I look into the deep red rose
Which throws a heavenly scent
It lures the eye to deep inside
Which is its own intent.

I swear I see a fairy there
With wings that fan the petals
She smiles at me and scatters dust
Her fairy dust that settles!

And all at once I smile for joy
And feel so very blessed
To witness this, I surely feel
More lucky than the rest

So in your garden, do be sure
To watch, and be aware
Your soft footfall may waken up
A fairy dwelling there.

Jane Windsor

Bagledon

Have you heard of Bagledon
A special cat he was,
Not tortoiseshell nor tabby
But, green with yellow paws,
Well, that was on a Tuesday
Some days he was quite pale,
On Sundays, he was scarlet red
With a glowing orange tail!
Then when he was feeling blue
He might be shocking pink,
When coloured all invisible
He'd not be where you'd think.
To find him put a little milk
In a saucer on the floor,
Watch the milk fill up inside
And . . . there he'd be, once more.

Zydha Hart

The Duckling That Wasn't

Mother Mallard stirred in her cosy nest in the flax bordering the little lake. Something was happening in the downy warmth beneath her. She carefully rose to stretch her cramped legs, and looked at her small clutch of eggs. She wondered why one of her lovely eggs was larger than the others. It was three weeks since she had laid them and she knew it could not be hers.

She noticed that her own eggs were beginning to crack and she thought she heard cheeping sounds. She settled down to wait for her babies to appear, wondering why the larger egg was not cracking. *I can wait one more day,* she thought, then settled down to wait.

During that night, nestling cosily in the safety of the flax bush she sensed that the large egg was hatching but she would wait until daylight to have a look.

Next morning at dawn she could wait no longer, she rose to greet her new family. Five downy brown-coloured babies cheeped excitedly at her but the strange one puzzled her. She had a longer neck, her colour was paler, and she did not cheep like her brothers and sisters. She was silent. 'Oh well, we cannot all be beautiful,' said Mother Mallard as she led them down to the water.

'And now children, off to sleep; tomorrow I will tell you about the strange duckling which was a beautiful white swan baby which we call a cygnet, and which cannot talk.'

Patrick Glasson

Mummy's Magic Books

When William read his books, something special happened. By turning the pages back and forth, William could turn the night back into day, he could stop the rain, and send flowers back into the ground.

Mummy kept her books in the kitchen. When William was hungry, she would open the books and make his tea appear. William thought they must be magic books. More than anything, William wanted to read Mummy's books.

Once Mummy said, 'Mummy is going upstairs, William. Play with your toys until I am back.' Through the doorway, William could see Mummy's books on the low kitchen shelf. He rolled onto his tummy and crawled towards them.

William tugged on a book. It fell to the floor - *thud* - And he opened it and chuckled at the funny shapes and bright colours. Suddenly the other books began to make a noise - *shhhh …*

Clunk! Crash! Books began toppling around him. He tried turning the pages backwards, to put the books back, but they kept on toppling! William was frightened.

Suddenly Mummy picked him up. She whispered, 'You must not play with Mummy's books.' She took him to his playroom and went to tidy up. So the magic in Mummy's books was too powerful for him. It must be grown-up magic, which only Mummy could do.

He turned the pages of his book, watching the sun come up, and he made it go down again.

Jeremy Davies

Drizzle Rain

The turkey is a bird
And I've often wondered why
I've seen it flap its wings
But I've never seen it fly

I've seen it leave the ground
For a moment or maybe two
But never soar up high
Like other birds do

There lives in Hector's Hollow
A turkey called Drizzle Rain
Who flew to America
As a passenger on a plane

Drizzle was born
On the twenty-first of May
His parents named him Drizzle
Because it rained all day

Drizzle was a clever turkey
Who listened and learned fast
He even went to school
And came top of his class

Drizzle loved Hector's Hollow
Living near the river and the sea
But he longed to see America
And the Statue of Liberty

Drizzle's dream came true
One bright and sunny day
His dad gave him a ticket
To fly to the USA

America was indeed
The land of opportunity and sun
Drizzle rode with the cowboys
And had lots of fun

Drizzle thought he'd go to Hollywood
Perhaps become a star
But he couldn't afford the bus fare
Let alone hire a car

So Drizzle set out on foot
Worked and saved along the way
Until he arrived in Hollywood
Almost a year to the day

Thirsty and famished
Drizzle came across a sign
Eat and drink as much as you like
For a dollar and a dime

A limousine was passing
Its owner cried, 'Stop the car
See that handsome turkey
With my help he'll go far'

Drizzle was eating a doughnut
When in walked Candy Barr
A famous Hollywood producer
Who promised to make him a star

Addicted to food
Candy ate day and night
Or chewed on a cigar
He never set alight

But Candy was a genius
Sharp in every way
Drizzle was never out of work
Not even for a day

Drizzle appeared in a western
With gunfights galore
And found he could run
Much faster than before

Drizzle won fame and fortune
And deserved all he got
He met some friendly Indians
And liked them quite a lot

But Drizzle was missing his family
So with the blessing of Candy Barr
He flew back home to England
A rich and famous star

In America there are cities
With skyscrapers by the score
Where people in their thousands
Swarm like ants on the floor

There are deserts in America
Vast areas of land
With very little water
And an awful lot of sand

In the desert there are scorpions
Grumpy rattlers ready to bite
The sun will roast you in the daytime
And leave you to freeze at night

Drizzle once met a buzzard
Called Joey Valentine
Lucky for young Drizzle
Joey wasn't hungry at the time

There's so much more to America
Than any one person can tell
But don't you think for a turkey
Drizzle did exceptionally well?

R V Chamberlain

Happily Ever After

Happily ever after
Fairy tales say
Happily ever after
Not so good today
I wish I had a happy day today

I try and try
But with no use
Happily ever after
Not so good today
But suddenly
I saw my future ahead of me
I said everything changed in front of me
I saw I had a very good family
I also saw that I had the best of friends
And that's what you call
Happily ever after.

Amr Abdelbaset (10)

Imagination Garden

In Imagination Garden
Things can be such fun,
The grass is super springy;
There's a smiling, happy sun,
The multicoloured flowers
Keep dancing in the breeze
And music plays forever
At the top of the trees.

It's a place that you can go to,
If you're feeling sad and blue
And no one else knows where it is;
It's a secret just for you,
There are many places to hide in
When you don't want to be found
And wondrous food of every kind
Growing from the ground.

There is a little gentle river
Which runs the whole way through,
With its sparkling blue water
Making everything anew,
So stay a while to play there
You can shout, laugh or cry,
Let Imagination Garden transport you
In a wink of an eye.

Tracey Lynn Birchall

The Author Of Life

Life is like writing a book,
And you are the proud author.
Life weaves out like a story,
Where you pick very word.

Unexpected things may happen throughout the years,
Things that just came about without any warning.
But remember that they were only hidden words,
Just waiting to spring onto the page.

Let me state the disadvantages in life.
You can't rub anything out, or erase it from the story.
All you can do is balance the odds and
Make up for anything you did not mean to write.

Good luck and bad luck, like coincidence,
Are minor sentences on the pages,
They do not get in the way . . . unless you let them,
The book is how you choose it to be.

When fully healthy people are just staying in,
Not doing much for days on end
They're not particularly lazy or boring,
They have writers block, they do not know what to do next.

Let your family be your pages,
Let your good friends be your ink.
Your life is the subject
And let God be your guiding hand.

Step through your tale, unravel what you think best.
The beginning, the middle and end are all yours to write.
No one can steal your ideas, more than live your life for you.
Billions of stories are written every day,
Write yours along with them.

Stories are strange, strange things,
They do not begin at the beginning,
They do not end at the end.

They are a never-ending adventure.
Confined to being told in words,
Trapped to white pages,
Locked between two hard covers.

However, lives do have an end.
Although our souls may live on forever.

When at last you write the final words,
Your pages come to a conclusion.
Close the back cover of your book,
And leave your novel behind.

Then step forth into the unknown . . .

Claire Bamford

Little One

Wake up, little one
I hope you slept okay
Why don't you enjoy yourself
It's the start of a new day.

Laugh, little one
I love the sound you make
I'll even give you a treat
Do you want some cake?

Walk, little one
We can even go to the shop
Don't worry about falling
As I'll be here if you drop.

Sing, little one
It's going to be great
You're going to turn 2 tomorrow
I bet you just can't wait.

Cry, little one
Tell me what you need
I'll get you anything you want
Do you need to feed?

Sleep, little one
I shall keep the monster at bay
He won't get the better of me
I'll ask him to go away.

Faiza Osman

The Harbinger And The Jester

Twinkle, twinkle shimmer his boots
In fun, in play are his roots
He growls like a bear, he makes play
Skip and trot he does along the path that day
'What whence I came, I laugh merrily,
Come red robin, hum away tweet tweetily
La-di-da, la-di-da fiddle may come
Feel my song become hum to the drum, drum'

Those were the words he sang on that road
In laughter, under sun, where no fear abode
His shoes were bells, they sang the sweetest tune
A story they told of love in the moon
And he spun and twinkled and danced at play
As if his soul had wings that day
But darkness filled up, no matter his will
The sun went down, it had its fill

'Tra-la-la, tra-la-la, come out sweet moon
Where you are, where you are, you shimmering bafoon
I stamp my feet, I will twinkle my bell-bells
You must light my path for all to be well!'
So he sung that merry tune that jasmine night
Until the birds of day with joy took flight
They formed shapes of flowers, ribbons and bows
And he clapped and shouted with every pose

But the moon did not come out, nor light his path
She cowered in fear from the Harbinger's wrath
For the moon's beauty many a princess swore
The Harbinger, had whispered death afore
'Moon, do not light up, do not seek this prince
I will bleed you dry, until your suitors wince
I will seek him out, do not take flight
Let my eyes alone take up his sight.'

And so the Harbinger, red fire and fury
Set out that night as promised duly
Long her hair of centuries made
But that fire's red tresses could not fade
The air it reeked of the heat she bore
As if cowering in lava on a volcano floor
Black shadows she wore, her robe of darkness
And her eyes broken promises of love and sweetness
She seemed as if to glide to the earth

Where the Jester played with merry and mirth
Until there she stood, bone's dust her illusion
To bring the Jester's life to sweet conclusion
She raised her hand, as if at play
And breathed a breath of life away
And as she was about to set death free
She saw the Jester at the birds with glee

His innocence and joy she felt her heart soften
Though fought she did at this sight
She watched him catch the robins at flight
His cheeks puffed out, his laughter booming
Until she could stand no longer to dooming
She turned in shame, and then saw her he did
He called out, ran behind an oak and hid
She stood frozen, breathless in fear unknown
And against herself, she slowly turned

'Come out sweet Jester, I mean you no ill.'
The world stood still.

'Harbinger I am, Harbinger I stay, Harbinger you see.
But please continue with glee.'

He peeked, his face set in fear
But in her eyes he glimpsed a tear
And then against him, he rushed to her side
As if always there, he did abide
He blew onto her soft skin
The tear it flew onto the wind

'Harbinger, I am Jester so true
Do not be blue, fore say
I will at you giggle, hahaha away!'
And he glimpsed her soul that day

They stared thus eye into eye
And the birds whispered as they flew by
'What? Why? No!' they cried
In fun he lives, in death she abides
But skin to skin, the Jester and Harbinger as one
And in mirth she played
And in sadness he weighed
Tasted thus and mixed from two
One heart they filled, and the birds they did woo
They soared into Heaven, and the Earth they kissed
But their free souls they sorely missed
Until one day they skipped as two
By day he fared, by night she dared

And in the twilight, they became one again bared
In twilight, they bore love and tore asunder
Until the world their passions admired in wonder
They became the raven, their love a jewel
They prayed for morn and night at bay so cruel
The moon held back as long as she dared
And watched the lovers in their love-making fared
And so and so became their lives so true
Harbinger and Jester, in world of midnight blue

And the Jester sang these worlds of old
To bring warmth to those so cold
'Tra-la-la she fires me, I play, I sing
I fly upon her raven's wing
Of fire, of stone, of dust she's made
Forsooth I say, my love she bade
Formed and formed, form me I say
Tra-la-la, tra-la-la come watch our day!'

And still the moon can hear his song
Through all the night, as he sleeps along
And Harbinger does her work of old
Taking warmth to make it cold
Listen, young ones, you will hear them play
Seek out their stars, at night and at day.

Natalie Williams

Growing Up

Poppy had been sitting on the edge of the grassy bank, swishing her feet in and out of the flowing water in the small brook not far from her nana's house. As a small child she would visit her grandparents' house when it was half term from school, Grandad would walk with her to the brook and he would let her take her shoes and socks off and sit down beside him on the grassy banking. He would then say, 'Away you go Poppy on your magic way, *swish swash* in the brook, I will just rest and watch you having fun.'

They would both laugh until one time Poppy slipped down into the water. She stayed where she sat. Grandad rushed to help her out. Holding tight to Grandad's hands she struggled to climb out with his help. He managed to pull her onto the grass. He just picked her up in his arms even though she was very wet, 'Come on lass let's get you home and in to some dry clothes. Your nan will think I have caught a fish, Poppy.'

Soon they were home. When they went into the kitchen Nan was laying the table for tea. When she saw the pair by the door, 'Grandad have you caught a fish for tea?' Everyone laughed.

'Come on Poppy let's get you into some dry clothes, then we can have our tea.'

Grandad sat down in his chair, started to read his paper. When Poppy's nan returned to the kitchen Grandad spoke to her. 'What a memory we have to keep forever dear?'

Poppy suddenly opened her eyes. She was dreaming now a teenager she had been thinking of her grandad. She was still swishing her feet in the brook, it was time to go to the house where Nan, now alone, would be waiting for her to return for tea. Poppy stood up, picked her shoes up and started to walk slowly back along the path.

As she arrived at the gate, she spoke out loud, 'Grandad how can I live happily ever after?' With tears in her eyes. Suddenly a white feather flew down in front of her. As she picked it up, she heard her grandad's voice saying, 'With memories Poppy, with memories.'

Poppy smiled. Yes she had plenty of memories

Nan was waiting by the door. 'Well love, had a nice time by the brook?'

'Yes Nan, with lots of memories to last forever.'

They both went into the house and Poppy closed the door.

Just like the past, her memories would last forever.

Dilys Hallam

Forward Poetry Information

We hope you have enjoyed reading this book - and that you will continue to enjoy it in the coming years.

If you like reading and writing poetry drop us a line, or give us a call, and we'll send you a free information pack.

Alternatively if you would like to order further copies of this book or any of our other titles, then please give us a call or log onto our website at www.forwardpoetry.co.uk

Forward Poetry Information
Remus House
Coltsfoot Drive
Peterborough
PE2 9BF
(01733) 890099